BLACK&DECKER®

ADVANCED
HOME WIRING

- Updated 2nd Edition
- New Circuits
- Outdoor Wiring

Creative Publishing
international

MINNEAPOLIS, MINNESOTA
www.creativepub.com

Creative Publishing
international

Copyright © 2009
Creative Publishing international, Inc.
400 First Avenue North, Suite 300
Minneapolis, Minnesota 55401
1-800-328-0590
www.creativepub.com

Printed at R.R. Donnelley

10 9 8 7 6 5 4 3

Library of Congress Cataloging-in-Publication Data

Advanced home wiring. -- Updated 2nd ed.
    p. cm.
  "Black & Decker."
  Includes index.
  Summary: "Includes advanced wiring projects such as installing a
subpanel and wiring an outbuilding"--Provided by publisher.
  ISBN-13: 978-1-58923-414-7 (soft cover)
  ISBN-10: 1-58923-414-6 (soft cover)
  1. Electric wiring, Interior--Amateurs' manuals.
  TK9901.A34 2009
  621.319'24--dc22
                            2008037848

President/CEO: Ken Fund
VP for Sales & Marketing: Kevin Hamric

Home Improvement Group

Publisher: Bryan Trandem
Managing Editor: Tracy Stanley
Senior Editor: Mark Johanson

Creative Director: Michele Lanci-Altomare
Senior Design Managers: Jon Simpson, Brad Springer
Design Manager: James Kegley

Lead Photographer: Steve Galvin
Photo Coordinator: Joanne Wawra
Shop Manager: Bryan McLain
Shop Assistant: Cesar Fernandez Rodriguez

Production Managers: Linda Halls, Laura Hokkanen

Page Layout Artist: Danielle Smith
Photographer: Andrea Rugg
Shop Help: Scott Boyd, David Hartley

Advanced Home Wiring
Created by: The Editors of Creative Publishing international, Inc., in cooperation with Black & Decker.
Black & Decker® is a trademark of The Black & Decker Corporation and is used under license.

NOTICE TO READERS

For safety, use caution, care, and good judgment when following the procedures described in this book. The publisher and Black & Decker cannot assume responsibility for any damage to property or injury to persons as a result of misuse of the information provided.

The techniques shown in this book are general techniques for various applications. In some instances, additional techniques not shown in this book may be required. Always follow manufacturers' instructions included with products, since deviating from the directions may void warranties. The projects in this book vary widely as to skill levels required: some may not be appropriate for all do-it-yourselfers, and some may require professional help.

Consult your local building department for information on building permits, codes, and other laws as they apply to your project.

2/09
6/09

Contents

Advanced Home Wiring

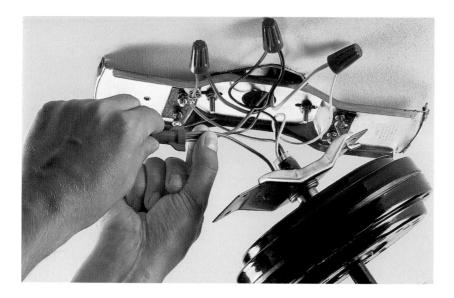

Introduction

This book is intended for the home DIYer ready to go to the next step, after having mastered basic electrical repairs like replacing switches, receptacles, and light fixtures.

It presumes that you already know a little bit about how electricity works, but are now considering adding entire new circuits to your system, or perhaps are even thinking about upgrading your entire electrical system.

As readers of the previous edition can attest, *Advanced Home Wiring* can save you literally thousands of dollars. It includes all the essential information for installing new wiring in your house—up to and including wiring a brand-new room addition from start to finish.

This edition is based on the National Electrical Code (NEC) approved for the dates 2008 through 2011. If you are using this book after these dates, you should check with local authorities for any recent changes in your area. Major changes to the Electrical Code are rare, and often are more applicable to commercial wiring than to residential, but it is still your responsibility to make sure your work complies with the legal requirements at the time you are doing the installation.

In addition to subtle updates to make the new edition current with today's Electrical Code, this book contains information on installing low-voltage surface ribbon wiring, which was not found in the previous edition.

In the opening chapter, "Planning a Wiring Project," you'll find out which Electrical Code requirements apply to your project, as well as how to work with your local electrical inspector. You'll see how to evaluate your existing electrical capacity and power usage, and determine the needs of the circuits you're adding. A series of circuit maps shows you the most common wiring layouts—a favorite feature with readers of the previous edition.

In "Tools, Materials & Techniques," you'll learn about the most current materials, as well as receive a review of general techniques for installing wiring.

Finally, three major wiring demonstrations show you how to install new wiring in some common applications. "Wiring a Room Addition" presents information applicable to a renovated attic, basement, or a newly constructed room addition. "Wiring a Remodeled Kitchen" focuses on the many dedicated specialty circuits required by the modern kitchen. "Installing Outdoor Wiring" shows you how to get power to any outdoor location, like a deck, garden shed, or detached garage.

Advanced Home Wiring helps take the mystery out of installing new circuits, and is sure to become an essential addition to your home improvement library.

Planning a Wiring Project

Careful planning of a wiring project ensures you will have plenty of power for present and future needs. Whether you are adding circuits in a room addition, wiring a remodeled kitchen, or adding an outdoor circuit, consider all possible ways the space might be used, and plan for enough electrical service to meet peak needs.

For example, when wiring a room addition, remember that the way a room is used can change. In a room used as a spare bedroom, a single 15-amp circuit provides plenty of power, but if you ever choose to convert the same room to a family recreation space, you will need additional circuits.

When wiring a remodeled kitchen, it is a good idea to install circuits for an electric oven and countertop range, even if you do not have these electric appliances. Installing these circuits now makes it easy to convert from gas to electric appliances at a later date.

A large wiring project adds a considerable load to your main electrical service. In about 25 percent of all homes, some type of service upgrade is needed before new wiring can be installed. For example, many homeowners will need to replace an older 60-amp electrical service with a new service rated for 100 amps or more. This is a job for a licensed electrician but is well worth the investment. In other cases, the existing main service provides adequate power, but the main circuit breaker panel is too full to hold any new circuit breakers. In this case it is necessary to install a circuit breaker subpanel to provide room for hooking up added circuits. Installing a subpanel is a job most homeowners can do themselves (page 40).

This chapter gives an easy five-step method for determining your electrical needs and planning new circuits.

Five Steps for Planning a Wiring Project

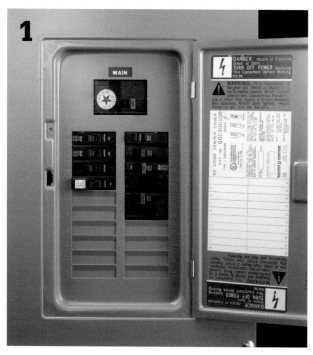

1

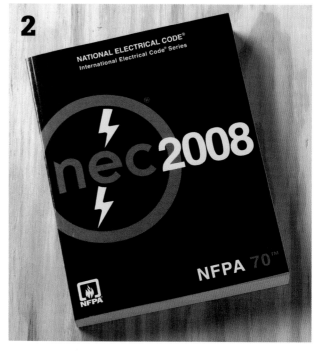

2

Examine your main service (page 8). The amp rating of the electrical service and the size of the circuit breaker panel will help you determine if a service upgrade is needed.

Learn about codes (page 9). The National Electrical Code (NEC), and local electrical codes and building codes, provide guidelines for determining how much power and how many circuits your home needs. Your local electrical inspector can tell you which regulations apply to your job.

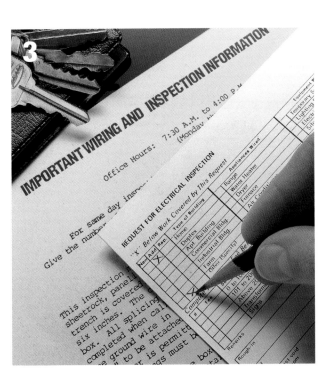

Prepare for inspections (page 10). Remember that your work must be reviewed by your local electrical inspector. When planning your wiring project, always follow the inspector's guidelines for quality workmanship.

Evaluate electrical loads (pages 12 to 13). New circuits put an added load on your electrical service. Make sure that total load of the existing wiring and the planned new circuits does not exceed the main service capacity.

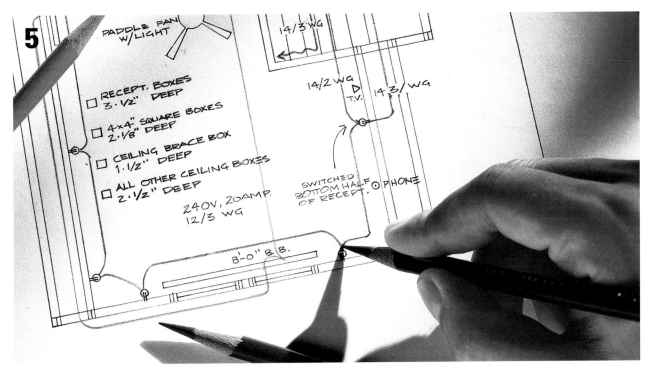

Draw a wiring diagram and get a permit (pages 14 to 15). This wiring plan will help you organize your work.

Examine Your Service Panel

The first step in planning a new wiring project is to look in your main circuit breaker panel and find the size of the service by reading the amperage rating on the main circuit breaker. As you plan new circuits and evaluate electrical loads, knowing the size of the main service helps you determine if you need a service upgrade.

Also look for open circuit breaker slots in the panel. The number of open slots will determine if you need to add a circuit breaker subpanel.

Find the service size by opening the main service panel and reading the amp rating printed on the main circuit breaker. In most cases, 100-amp service provides enough power to handle the added loads of projects like the ones shown in this book. A service rated for 60 amps or less may need to be upgraded.

Older service panels use fuses instead of circuit breakers. Have an electrician replace this type of panel with a circuit breaker panel that provides enough power and enough open breaker slots for the new circuits you are planning.

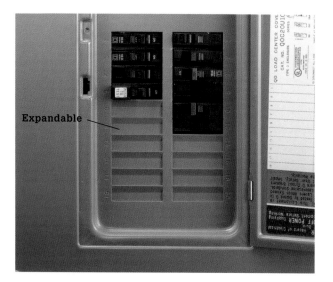

Look for open circuit breaker slots in the main circuit breaker panel or in a circuit breaker subpanel, if your home already has one. You will need one open slot for each 120-volt circuit you plan to install and two slots for each 240-volt circuit. If your main circuit breaker panel has no open breaker slots, install a subpanel (page 40) to provide room for connecting new circuits.

Learn About Codes

To ensure public safety, your community requires that you get a permit to install new wiring and have the completed work reviewed by an appointed inspector. Electrical inspectors use the National Electrical Code (NEC) as the primary authority for evaluating wiring, but they also follow the local Building Code and Electrical Code standards.

As you begin planning new circuits, call or visit your local electrical inspector and discuss the project with him. The inspector can tell you which of the national and local code requirements apply to your job, and may give you a packet of information summarizing these regulations. Later, when you apply to the inspector for a work permit, he will expect you to understand the local guidelines as well as a few basic National Electrical Code requirements.

The National Electrical Code is a set of standards that provides minimum safety requirements for wiring installations. It is revised every three years. The national code requirements for the projects shown in this book are thoroughly explained on the following pages. For more information, you can find copies of the current NEC, as well as a number of excellent handbooks based on the NEC, at libraries and bookstores.

In addition to being the final authority of code requirements, inspectors are electrical professionals with years of experience. Although they have busy schedules, most inspectors are happy to answer questions and help you design well-planned circuits.

Basic Electrical Code Requirements

Electrical Code requirements for living areas: Living areas need at least one 15-amp or 20-amp basic lighting/receptacle circuit for each 600 sq. ft. of living space and should have a dedicated circuit for each type of permanent appliance, like an air conditioner, computer, or a group of baseboard heaters and within 6 ft. of any door opening. Receptacles on basic lighting/receptacle circuits should be spaced no more than 12 ft. apart. Many electricians and electrical inspectors recommend even closer spacing. Any wall more than 24" wide also needs a receptacle. Every room should have a wall switch at the point of entry to control either a ceiling light or plug-in lamp. Kitchens and bathrooms must have a ceiling-mounted light fixture.

Prepare for Inspections

Electrical inspectors who issue the work permit for your wiring project will also visit your home to review the work. Make sure to allow time for these inspections as you plan the project. For most projects, inspectors make two visits.

The first inspection, called the rough-in, is done after the cables are run between the boxes but before the insulation, wallboard, switches, and fixtures are installed. The second inspection, called the final, is done after the walls and ceilings are finished and all electrical connections are made.

When preparing for the rough-in inspection, make sure the area is neat. Sweep up sawdust and clean up any pieces of scrap wire or cable insulation. Before inspecting the boxes and cables, inspectors will check to make sure all plumbing and other mechanical work is completed. Some electrical inspectors will ask to see your building and plumbing permits.

At the final inspection, inspectors check random boxes to make sure the wire connections are correct.

If they see good workmanship at the selected boxes, the inspection will be over quickly. However, if they spot a problem, inspectors may choose to inspect every connection.

Inspectors have busy schedules, so it is a good idea to arrange for an inspection several days or weeks in advance. In addition to basic compliance with code, inspectors expect your work to meet their own standards for quality. When you apply for a work permit, make sure you understand what the inspectors will look for during inspections.

You cannot put new circuits into use legally until an inspector approves them at the final inspection. Because inspectors are responsible for the safety of all wiring installations, their approval means that your work meets professional standards. If you have planned carefully and done your work well, electrical inspections are routine visits that give you confidence in your own skills.

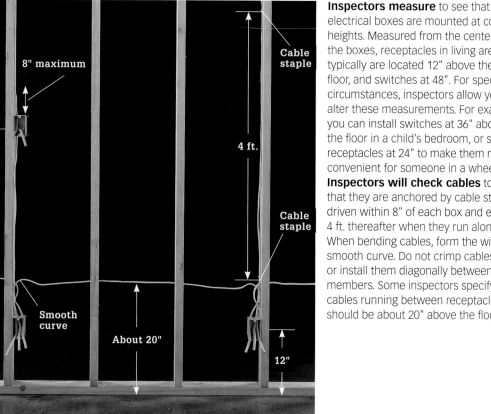

Inspectors measure to see that electrical boxes are mounted at consistent heights. Measured from the center of the boxes, receptacles in living areas typically are located 12" above the finished floor, and switches at 48". For special circumstances, inspectors allow you to alter these measurements. For example, you can install switches at 36" above the floor in a child's bedroom, or set receptacles at 24" to make them more convenient for someone in a wheelchair.

Inspectors will check cables to see that they are anchored by cable staples driven within 8" of each box and every 4 ft. thereafter when they run along studs. When bending cables, form the wire in a smooth curve. Do not crimp cables sharply or install them diagonally between framing members. Some inspectors specify that cables running between receptacle boxes should be about 20" above the floor.

What Inspectors Look For

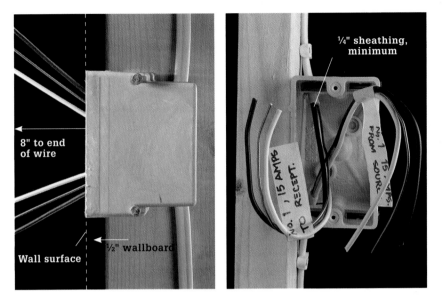

Electrical box faces should extend past the front of framing members so the boxes will be flush with finished walls (left). Inspectors will check to see that all boxes are large enough for the wires they contain. Cables should be cut and stripped back so that 8" of usable length extends past the front of the box, and so that at least ¼" of sheathing reaches into the box (right). Label all cables to show which circuits they serve: inspectors recognize this as a mark of careful work. The labels also simplify the final hookups after the wallboard is installed.

Install an isolated-ground circuit and receptacle if recommended by your inspector. An isolated-ground circuit protects sensitive electronic equipment against tiny current fluctuations and interference. Electronics also should be protected by either a plug-in surge protector or a whole-house surge arrestor.

Heating & Air Conditioning Chart ▸
(compiled from manufacturers' literature)

Room addition living area	Recommended total heating rating	Recommended circuit size	Recommended air-conditioner rating	Recommended circuit size
100 sq. ft.	900 watts	15-amp (240 volts)	5,000 BTU	15-amp (120 volts)
150 sq. ft.	1,350 watts		6,000 BTU	
200 sq. ft.	1,800 watts		7,000 BTU	
300 sq. ft.	2,700 watts		9,000 BTU	
400 sq. ft.	3,600 watts	20-amp (240 volts)	10,500 BTU	
500 sq. ft.	4,500 watts	30-amp (240 volts)	11,500 BTU	20-amp (120 volts)
800 sq. ft.	7,200 watts	two 20-amp	17,000 BTU	15-amp (240 volts)
1,000 sq. ft.	9,000 watts	two 30-amp	21,000 BTU	20-amp (240 volts)

Electric heating and air conditioning for a new room addition will be checked by an inspector. Determine your heating and air-conditioning needs by finding the total area of the living space. Choose electric heating units with a combined wattage rating close to the chart recommendation above. Choose an air conditioner with a BTU rating close to the chart recommendation for your room size. *Note: These recommendations are for homes in moderately cool climates, sometimes referred to as Zone 4 regions. Cities in Zone 4 include Denver, Chicago, and Boston. In more severe climates, check with your electrical inspector or energy agency to learn how to find heating and air-conditioning needs.*

Evaluate Electrical Loads

Before drawing a plan and applying for a work permit, make sure your home's electrical service provides enough power to handle the added load of the new circuits. In a safe wiring system, the current drawn by fixtures and appliances never exceeds the main service capacity.

To evaluate electrical loads, use a work sheet or whatever evaluation method is recommended by your electrical inspector. Include the load for all existing wiring as well as that for proposed new wiring when making your evaluation.

Most of the light fixtures and plug-in appliances in your home are evaluated as part of general allowances for basic lighting/receptacle circuits and small-appliance circuits. However, appliances that are permanently installed require their own dedicated circuits. The electrical loads for these appliances are added in separately when evaluating wiring.

If your evaluation shows that the load exceeds the main service capacity, you must have an electrician upgrade the main service before you can install new wiring. An electrical service upgrade is a worthwhile investment that improves the value of your home and provides plenty of power for present and future wiring projects.

Amperage ▸

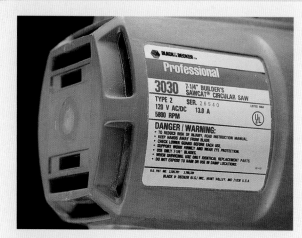

Amperage rating can be used to find the wattage of an appliance. Multiply the amperage by the voltage of the circuit. For example, a 13-amp, 120-volt circular saw is rated for 1,560 watts.

Amps × Volts	Total capacity	Safe capacity
15 A × 120 V =	1,800 watts	1,440 watts
20 A × 120 V =	2,400 watts	1,920 watts
25 A × 120 V =	3,000 watts	2,400 watts
30 A × 120 V =	3,600 watts	2,880 watts
20 A × 240 V =	4,800 watts	3,840 watts
30 A × 240 V =	7,200 watts	5,760 watts

Calculating Loads

Add 1,500 watts for each small appliance circuit required by the local electrical code. In most communities, three such circuits are required—two in the kitchen and one for the laundry—for a total of 4,500 watts. No further calculations are needed for appliances that plug into small-appliance or basic lighting/receptacle circuits.

If the nameplate gives the rating in kilowatts, find the watts by multiplying kilowatts times 1,000. If an appliance lists only amps, find watts by multiplying the amps times the voltage—either 120 or 240 volts.

Air-conditioning and heating appliances are not used at the same time, so figure in only the larger of these two numbers when evaluating your home's electrical load.

Outdoor receptacles and fixtures are not included in basic lighting calculations. When evaluating electrical loads, add in the nameplate wattage rating for each outdoor light fixture, and add in 180 watts for each outdoor receptacle. Receptacles and light fixtures in garages also are considered to be outdoor fixtures when evaluating loads.

Draw a Diagram & Get a Permit

Drawing a wiring diagram is the last step in planning a circuit installation. A detailed wiring diagram helps you get a work permit, makes it easy to create a list of materials, and serves as a guide for laying out circuits and installing cables and fixtures. Use the circuit maps on pages 18 to 33 as a guide for planning wiring configurations and cable runs. Bring the diagram and materials list when you visit electrical inspectors to apply for a work permit.

Never install new wiring without following your community's permit and inspection procedure. A work permit is not expensive, and it ensures that your work will be reviewed by a qualified inspector to guarantee its safety. If you install new wiring without the proper permit, an accident or fire traced to faulty wiring could cause your insurance company to discontinue your policy and could hurt the resale value of your home.

When electrical inspectors look over your wiring diagram, they will ask questions to see if you have a basic understanding of the electrical code and fundamental wiring skills. Some inspectors ask these questions informally, while others give a short written test. Inspectors may allow you to do some, but not all, of the work. For example, they may ask that all final circuit connections at the circuit breaker panel be made by a licensed electrician, while allowing you to do all other work.

A few communities allow you to install wiring only when supervised by an electrician. This means you can still install your own wiring but must hire an electrician to apply for the work permit and to check your work before inspectors review it. The electrician is held responsible for the quality of the job.

Remember that it is the inspectors' responsibility to help you do a safe and professional job. Feel free to call them with questions about wiring techniques or materials.

A detailed wiring diagram and a list of materials is required before electrical inspectors will issue a work permit. If blueprints exist for the space you are remodeling, start your electrical diagram by tracing the wall outlines from the blueprint. Use standard electrical symbols (next page) to clearly show all the receptacles, switches, light fixtures, and permanent appliances. Make a copy of the symbol key, and attach it to the wiring diagram for the inspectors' convenience. Show each cable run, and label its wire size and circuit amperage.

How to Draw a Wiring Plan

1

Draw a scaled diagram of the space you will be wiring, showing walls, doors, windows, plumbing pipes and fixtures, and heating and cooling ducts. Find the floor space by multiplying room length by width, and indicate this on the diagram. Do not include closets or storage areas when figuring space.

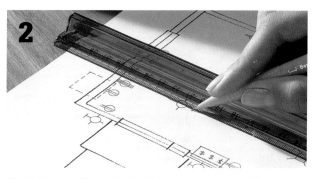

2

Mark the location of all switches, receptacles, light fixtures, and permanent appliances using the electrical symbols shown below. Where you locate these devices along the cable run determines how they are wired. Use the circuit maps on pages 18 to 33 as a guide for drawing wiring diagrams.

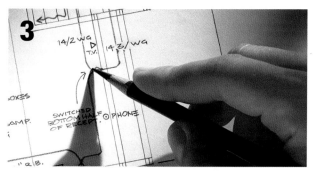

3

Draw in cable runs between devices. Indicate cable size and type, and the amperage of the circuits. Use a different-colored pencil for each circuit.

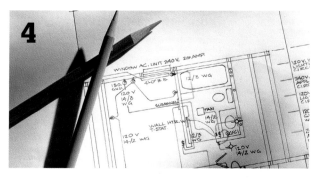

4

Identify the wattages for light fixtures and permanent appliances, and the type and size of each electrical box. On another sheet of paper, make a detailed list of all materials you will use.

Electrical Symbol Key ▸
(copy this key and attach it to your wiring plan)

	240-volt receptacle
	Isolated ground receptacle
	Duplex receptacle
	240-volt dryer receptacle
	Singleplex receptacle
	Fourplex receptacle
GFCI	GFCI duplex receptacle
	Switched receptacle
WP	Weatherproof receptacle
S_{TH}	Thermostat
S_P	Pilot-light switch
S	Single-pole switch
S_T	Timer switch
S_3	Three-way switch
J	Junction box
S	Ceiling pull switch
	Surface-mounted light fixture
R	Recessed light fixture
	Fluorescent light fixture
	Wall-mounted light fixture
WP	Weatherproof light fixture
CF	Ceiling fan
D	Electric door opener
BT	Low-voltage transformer
TV	Television jack
▶	Telephone outlet
D	Smoke detector
VF	Vent fan

2-WIRE CABLE

3-WIRE CABLE

To light

POWER CONTROLS
CORP.
SAN ANTONIO TEXAS

MOTOR/FAN
SPEED CONTROL

HI OFF

QUIET

72N
IND. CONT. EQ.

1.5 AMP   120
60 HZ   V.A.C.

XML 600-320

Circuit Maps

The arrangement of switches and appliances along an electrical circuit differs for every project. This means that the configuration of wires inside an electrical box can vary greatly, even when fixtures are identical.

The circuit maps on the following pages show the most common wiring variations for typical electrical devices. Most new wiring you install will match one or more of the maps shown. Find the maps that match your situation and use them to plan your circuit layouts.

The 120-volt circuits shown on the following pages are wired for 15 amps using 14-gauge wire and receptacles rated at 15 amps. If you are installing a 20-amp circuit, substitute 12-gauge cables and use receptacles rated for 20 amps.

In configurations where a white wire serves as a hot wire instead of a neutral, both ends of the wire are coded with black tape to identify it as hot. In addition, each of the circuit maps shows a box grounding screw. This grounding screw is required in all metal boxes, but plastic electrical boxes do not need to be grounded.

Note: For clarity, all grounding conductors in the circuit maps are colored green. In practice, the grounding wires inside sheathed cables usually are bare copper.

Common Household Circuits

1. 120-VOLT DUPLEX RECEPTACLES WIRED IN SEQUENCE

Use this layout to link any number of duplex receptacles in a basic lighting/receptacle circuit. The last receptacle in the cable run is connected like the receptacle shown at the right side of the circuit map below. All other receptacles are wired like the receptacle shown on the left side. Requires two-wire cables.

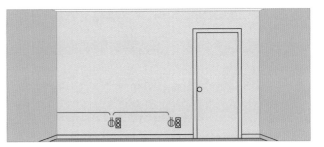

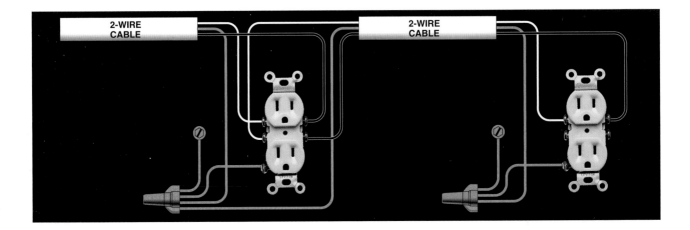

2. GFCI RECEPTACLES (SINGLE-LOCATION PROTECTION)

Use this layout when receptacles are within 6 ft. of a water source, like those in kitchens and bathrooms. To prevent nuisance tripping caused by normal power surges, ground fault circuit interruptors (GFCI) should be connected only at the line screw terminal so they protect a single location, not the fixtures on the load side of the circuit. Requires two-wire cables. Where a GFCI must protect other fixtures, use circuit map 3.

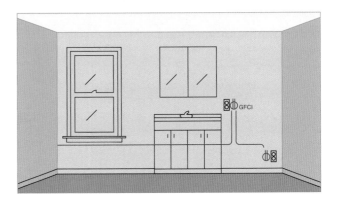

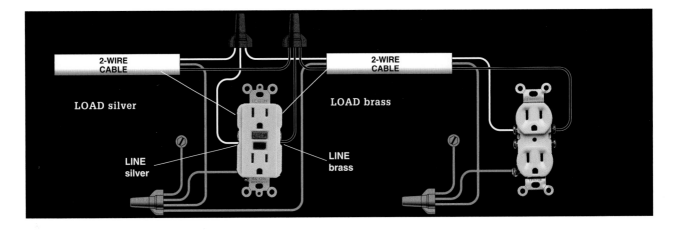

3. GFCI RECEPTACLE, SWITCH & LIGHT FIXTURE (WIRED FOR MULTIPLE-LOCATION PROTECTION)

In some locations, such as an outdoor circuit, it is a good idea to connect a GFCI receptacle so it also provides shock protection to the wires and fixtures that continue to the end of the circuit. Wires from the power source are connected to the line screw terminals; outgoing wires are connected to load screws. Requires two-wire cables.

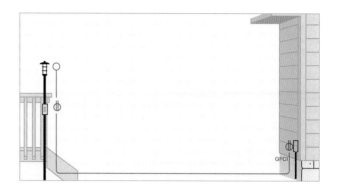

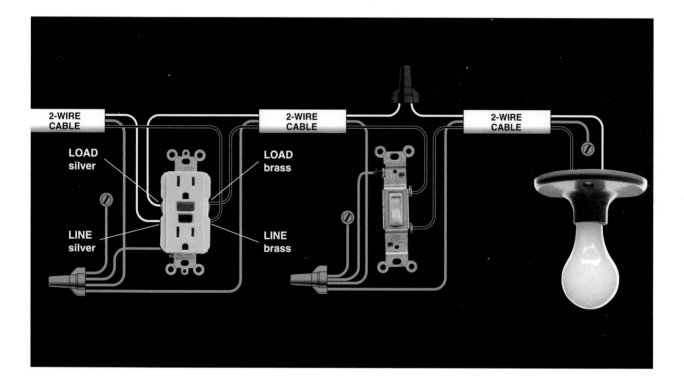

4. SINGLE-POLE SWITCH & LIGHT FIXTURE (LIGHT FIXTURE AT END OF CABLE RUN)

Use this layout for light fixtures in basic lighting/receptacle circuits throughout the home. It is often used as an extension to a series of receptacles (circuit map 1). Requires two-wire cables.

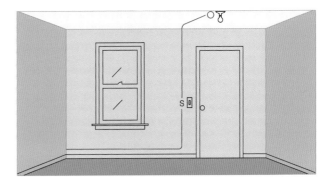

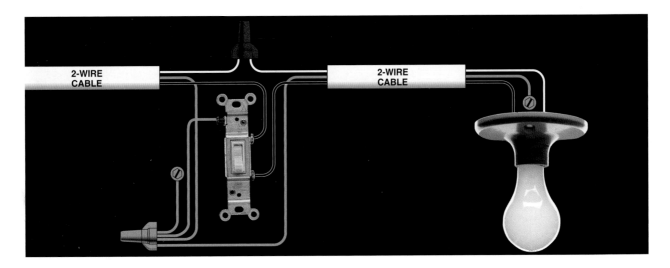

5. SINGLE-POLE SWITCH & LIGHT FIXTURE (SWITCH AT END OF CABLE RUN)

Use this layout, sometimes called a switch loop, where it is more practical to locate a switch at the end of the cable run. In the last length of cable, both insulated wires are hot; the white wire is tagged with black tape at both ends to indicate it is hot. Requires two-wire cables.

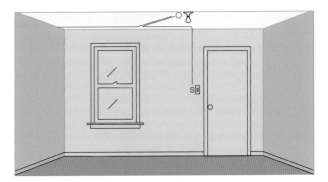

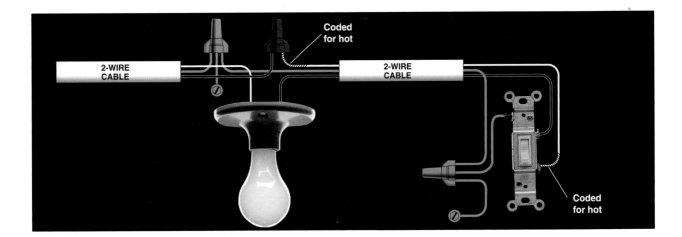

6. SINGLE-POLE SWITCH & TWO LIGHT FIXTURES (SWITCH BETWEEN LIGHT FIXTURES, LIGHT AT START OF CABLE RUN)

Use this layout when you need to control two fixtures from one single-pole switch and the switch is between the two lights in the cable run. Power feeds to one of the lights. Requires two-wire and three-wire cables.

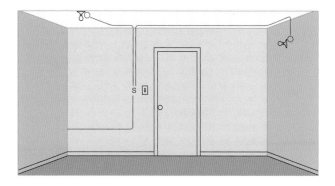

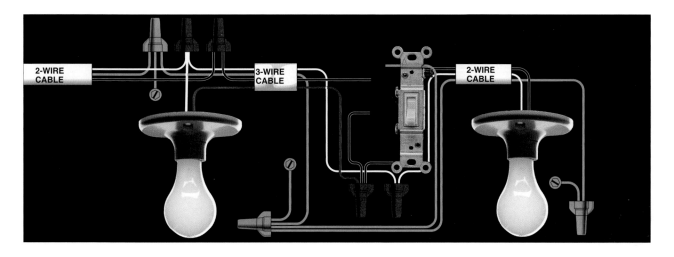

7. SINGLE-POLE SWITCH & LIGHT FIXTURE, DUPLEX RECEPTACLE (SWITCH AT START OF CABLE RUN)

Use this layout to continue a circuit past a switched light fixture to one or more duplex receptacles. To add multiple receptacles to the circuit, see circuit map 1. Requires two-wire and three-wire cables.

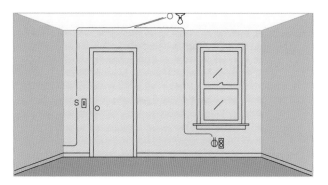

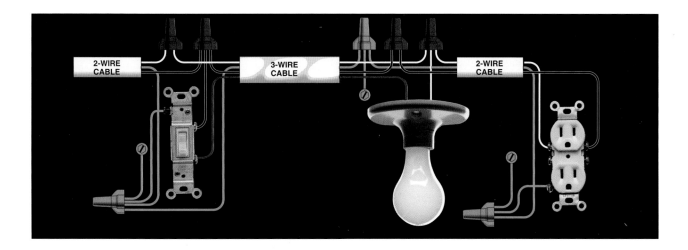

8. SWITCH-CONTROLLED SPLIT RECEPTACLE, DUPLEX RECEPTACLE (SWITCH AT START OF CABLE RUN)

This layout lets you use a wall switch to control a lamp plugged into a wall receptacle. This configuration is required by code for any room that does not have a switch-controlled ceiling fixture. Only the bottom half of the first receptacle is controlled by the wall switch; the top half of the receptacle and all additional receptacles on the circuit are always hot. Requires two-wire and three-wire cables.

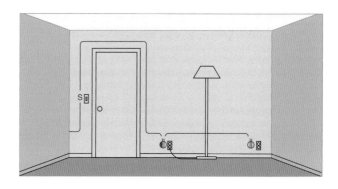

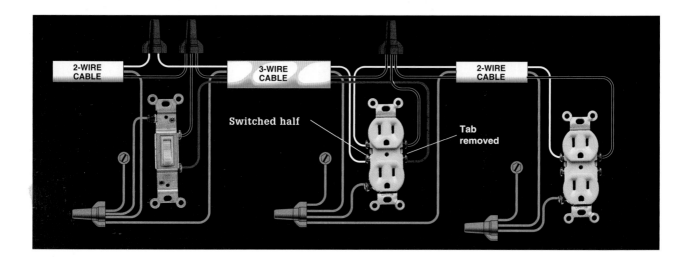

9. SWITCH-CONTROLLED SPLIT RECEPTACLE (SWITCH AT END OF CABLE RUN)

Use this switch loop layout to control a split receptacle (see circuit map 7) from an end-of-run circuit location. The bottom half of the receptacle is controlled by the wall switch, while the top half is always hot. White circuit wire attached to the switch is tagged with black tape to indicate it is hot. Requires two-wire cable.

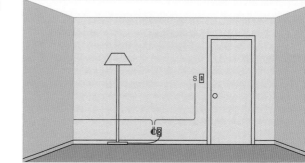

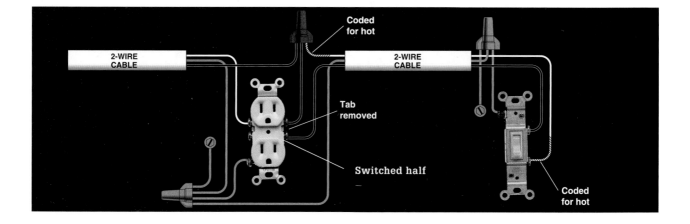

10. SWITCH-CONTROLLED SPLIT RECEPTACLE, DUPLEX RECEPTACLE (SPLIT RECEPTACLE AT START OF CABLE RUN)

Use this variation of circuit map 7 where it is more practical to locate a switch-controlled receptacle at the start of a cable run. Only the bottom half of the first receptacle is controlled by the wall switch; the top half of the receptacle, and all other receptacles on the circuit, are always hot. Requires two-wire cables.

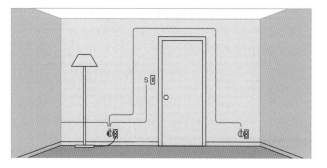

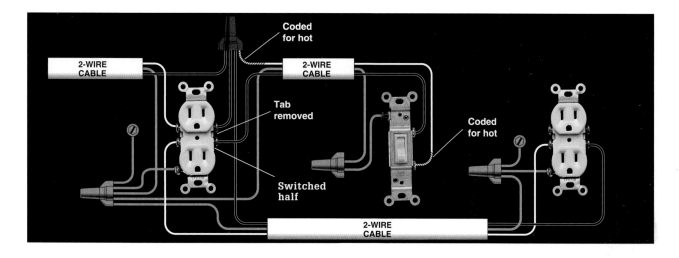

11. DOUBLE RECEPTACLE CIRCUIT WITH SHARED NEUTRAL WIRE (RECEPTACLES ALTERNATE CIRCUITS)

This layout features two 120-volt circuits wired with one three-wire cable connected to a double-pole circuit breaker. The black hot wire powers one circuit; the red wire powers the other. The white wire is a shared neutral that serves both circuits. When wired with 12/2 and 12/3 cable and receptacles rated for 20 amps, this layout can be used for the two small-appliance circuits required in a kitchen.

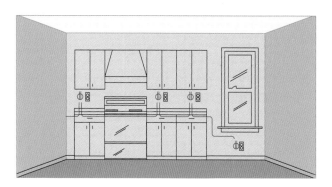

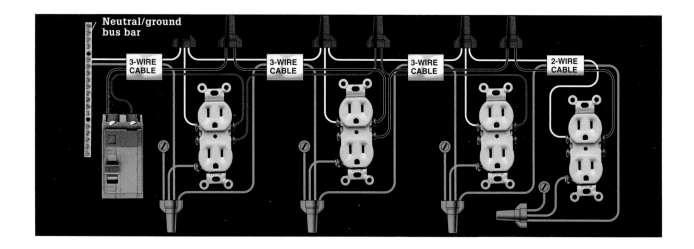

12. DOUBLE RECEPTACLE SMALL-APPLIANCE CIRCUIT WITH GFCIs & SHARED NEUTRAL WIRE

Use this layout variation of circuit map 10 to wire a double receptacle circuit when code requires that some of the receptacles be GFCIs. The GFCIs should be wired for single-location protection (see circuit map 2). Requires three-wire and two-wire cables.

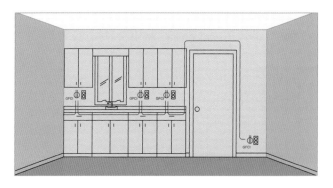

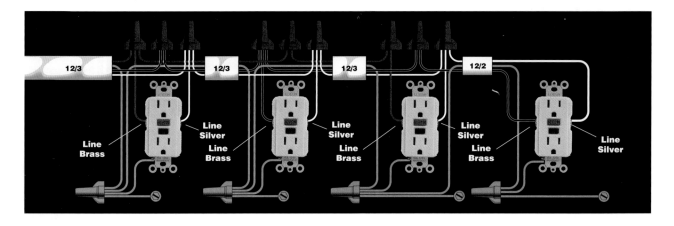

13. DOUBLE RECEPTACLE SMALL APPLIANCE CIRCUIT WITH GFCIs & SEPARATE NEUTRAL WIRES

If the room layout or local codes do not allow for a shared neutral wire, use this layout instead. The GFCIs should be wired for single-location protection (see circuit map 2). Requires two-wire cable.

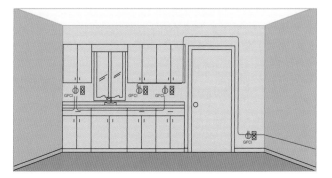

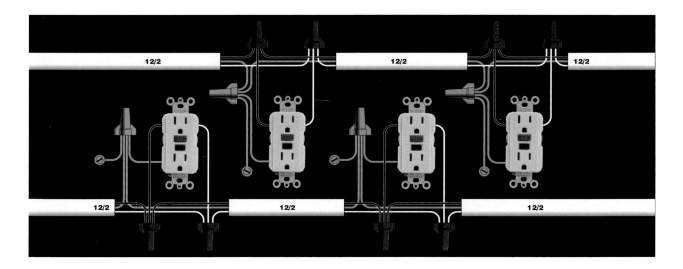

14. 120/240-VOLT RANGE RECEPTACLE

This layout is for a 50- or 60-amp, 120/240-volt dedicated appliance circuit wired with 6/3 cable, as required by code for a large kitchen range. The black and red circuit wires, connected to a double-pole circuit breaker in the circuit breaker panel, each bring 120 volts of power to the setscrew terminals on the receptacle. The white circuit wire attached to the neutral bus bar in the circuit breaker panel is connected to the neutral setscrew terminal on the receptacle.

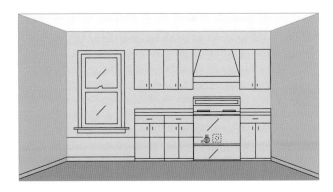

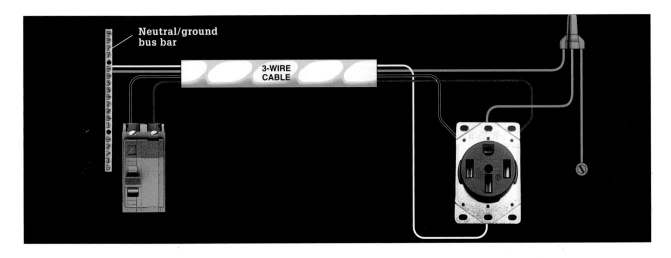

15. 240-VOLT BASEBOARD HEATERS, THERMOSTAT

This layout is typical for a series of 240-volt baseboard heaters controlled by a wall thermostat. Except for the last heater in the circuit, all heaters are wired as shown below. The last heater is connected to only one cable. The size of the circuit and cables are determined by finding the total wattage of all heaters. Requires two-wire cable.

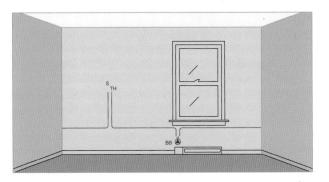

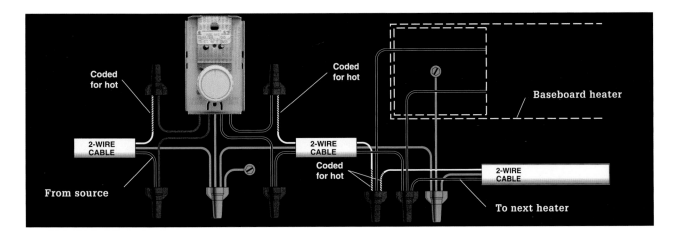

16. DEDICATED 120-VOLT COMPUTER CIRCUIT, ISOLATED-GROUND RECEPTACLE

This 15-amp isolated-ground circuit provides extra protection against surges and interference that can harm electronics. It uses 14/3 cable with the red wire serving as an extra grounding conductor. The red wire is tagged with green tape for identification. It is connected to the grounding screw on an isolated-ground receptacle and runs back to the grounding bus bar in the circuit breaker panel without touching any other house wiring.

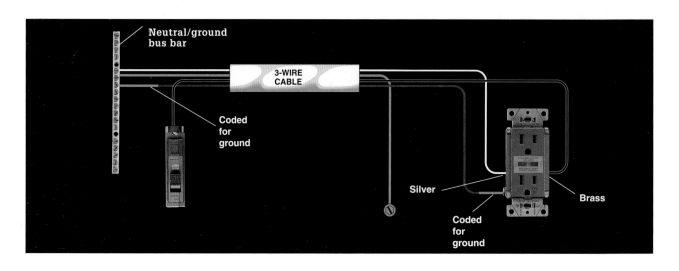

17. 240-VOLT APPLIANCE RECEPTACLE

This layout represents a 20-amp, 240-volt dedicated appliance circuit wired with 12/2 cable, as required by code for a large window air conditioner. Receptacles are available in both singleplex (shown) and duplex styles. The black and the white circuit wires connected to a double-pole breaker each bring 120 volts of power to the receptacle. The white wire is tagged with black tape to indicate it is hot.

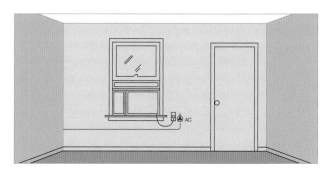

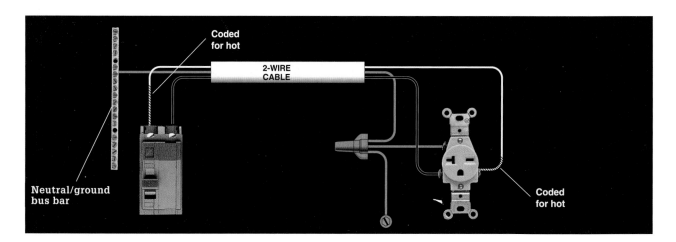

18. GANGED SINGLE-POLE SWITCHES CONTROLLING SEPARATE LIGHT FIXTURES

This layout lets you place two switches controlled by the same 120-volt circuit in one double-gang electrical box. A single feed cable provides power to both switches. A similar layout with two feed cables can be used to place switches from different circuits in the same box. Requires two-wire cable.

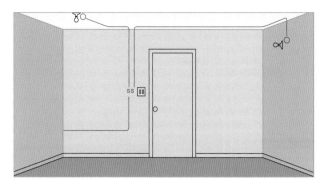

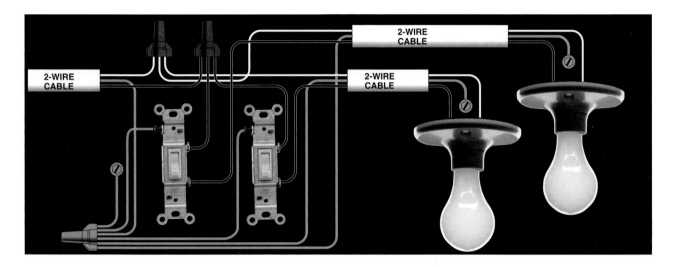

19. GANGED SWITCHES CONTROLLING A LIGHT FIXTURE AND A VENT FAN

This layout lets you place two switches controlled by the same 120-volt circuit in one double-gang electrical box. A single feed cable provides power to both switches. A standard switch controls the light fixture and a time-delay switch controls the vent fan.

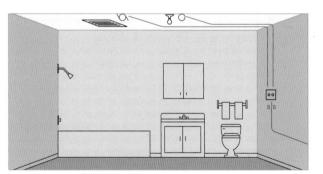

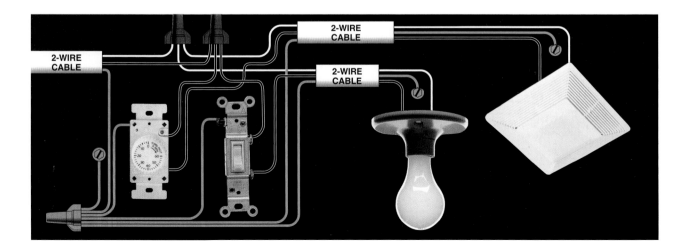

20. THREE-WAY SWITCHES & LIGHT FIXTURE (FIXTURE BETWEEN SWITCHES)

This layout for three-way switches lets you control a light fixture from two locations. Each switch has one common screw terminal and two traveler screws. Circuit wires attached to the traveler screws run between the two switches, and hot wires attached to the common screws bring current from the power source and carry it to the light fixture. Requires two-wire and three-wire cables.

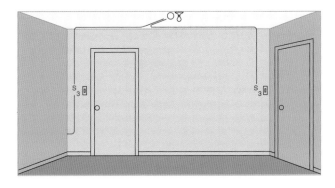

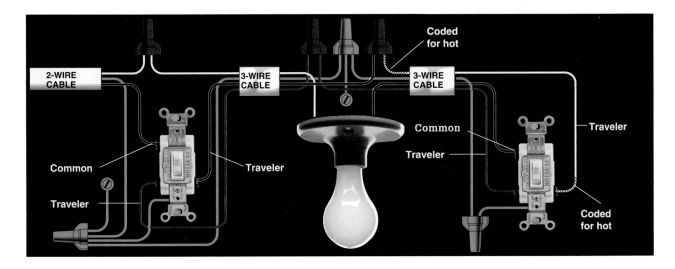

21. THREE-WAY SWITCHES & LIGHT FIXTURE (FIXTURE AT START OF CABLE RUN)

Use this layout variation of circuit map 19 where it is more convenient to locate the fixture ahead of the three-way switches in the cable run. Requires two-wire and three-wire cables.

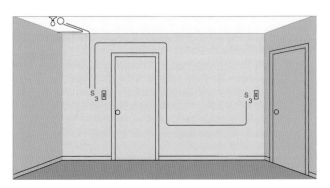

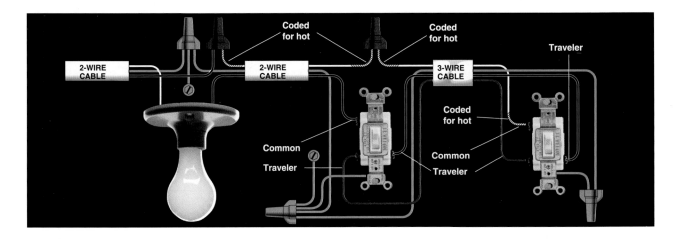

22. THREE-WAY SWITCHES & LIGHT FIXTURE (FIXTURE AT END OF CABLE RUN)

This variation of the three-way switch layout (circuit map 20) is used where it is more practical to locate the fixture at the end of the cable run. Requires two-wire and three-wire cables.

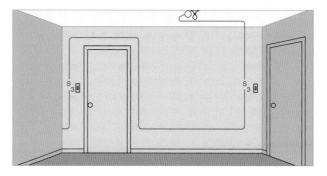

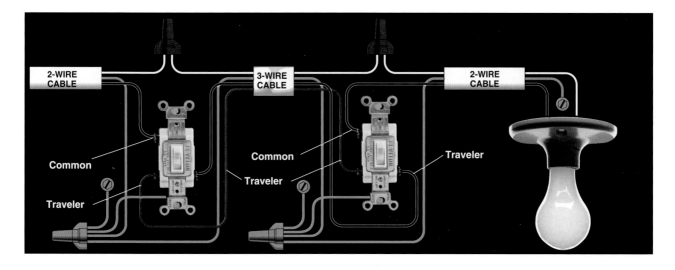

23. THREE-WAY SWITCHES & LIGHT FIXTURE WITH DUPLEX RECEPTACLE

Use this layout to add a receptacle to a three-way switch configuration (circuit map 21). Requires two-wire and three-wire cables.

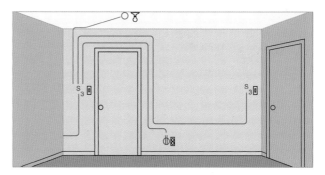

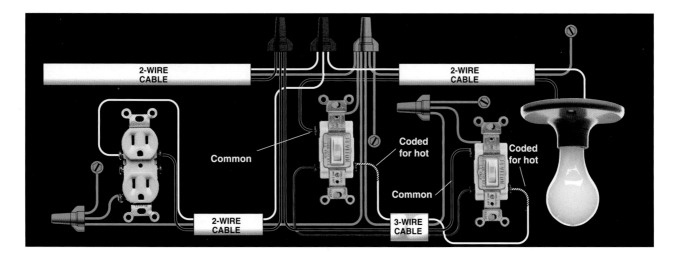

24. THREE-WAY SWITCHES & MULTIPLE LIGHT FIXTURES (FIXTURES BETWEEN SWITCHES)

This is a variation of circuit map 20. Use it to place multiple light fixtures between two three-way switches where power comes in at one of the switches. Requires two- and three-wire cable.

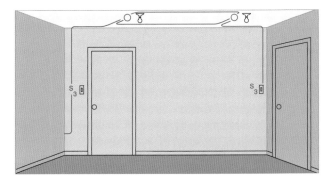

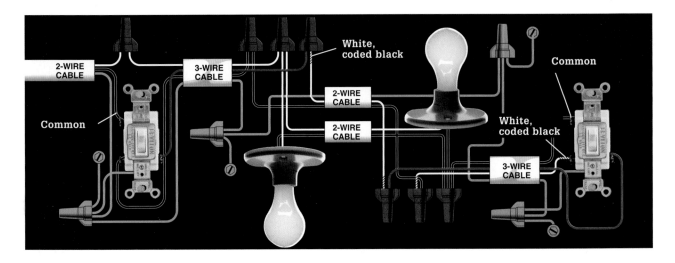

25. THREE-WAY SWITCHES & MULTIPLE LIGHT FIXTURES (FIXTURES AT START OF CABLE RUN)

This is a variation of circuit map 21. Use it to place multiple light fixtures at the beginning of a run controlled by two three-way switches. Power comes in at the first fixture. Requires two- and three-wire cable.

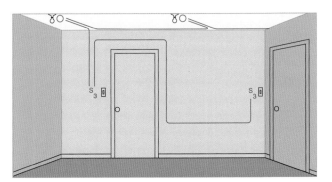

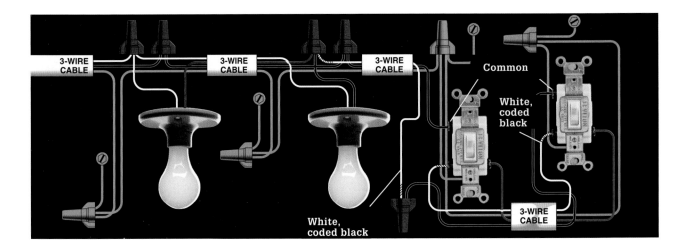

26. FOUR-WAY SWITCH & LIGHT FIXTURE (FIXTURE AT START OF CABLE RUN)

This layout lets you control a light fixture from three locations. The end switches are three-way and the middle is four-way. A pair of three-wire cables enter the box of the four-way switch. The white and red wires from one cable attach to the top pair of screw terminals (line 1) and the white and red wires from the other cable attaches to the bottom screw terminals (line 2). Requires two three-way switches and one four-way switch and two-wire and three-wire cables.

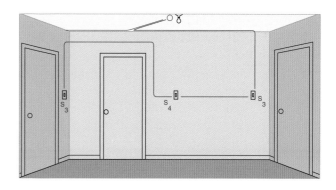

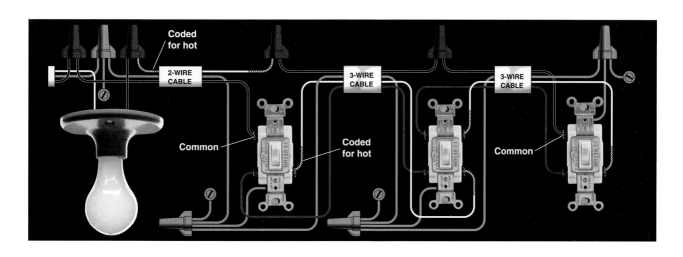

27. FOUR-WAY SWITCH & LIGHT FIXTURE (FIXTURE AT END OF CABLE RUN)

Use this layout variation of circuit map 26 where it is more practical to locate the fixture at the end of the cable run. Requires two three-way switches and one four-way switch and two-wire and three-wire cables.

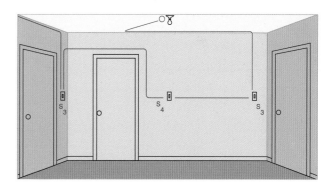

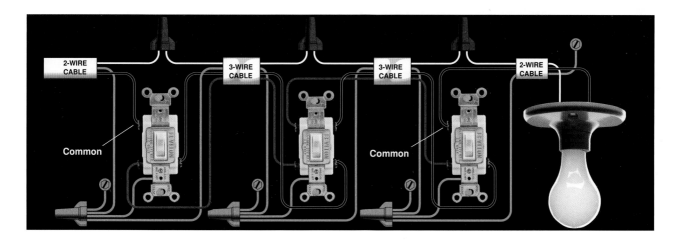

28. MULTIPLE FOUR-WAY SWITCHES CONTROLLING A LIGHT FIXTURE

This alternate variation of the four-way switch layout (circuit map 27) is used where three or more switches will control a single fixture. The outer switches are three-way and the middle are four-way. Requires two three-way switches and two four-way switches and two-wire and three-wire cables.

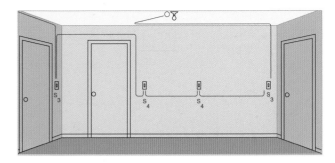

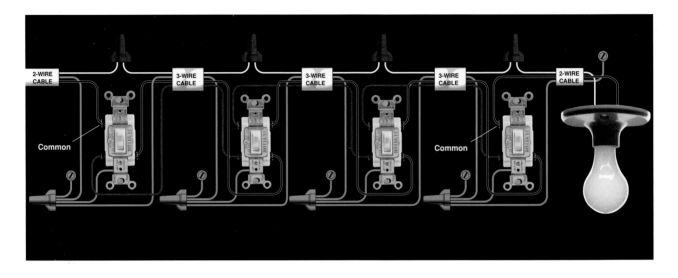

29. FOUR-WAY SWITCHES & MULTIPLE LIGHT FIXTURES

This variation of the four-way switch layout (circuit map 26) is used where two or more fixtures will be controlled from multiple locations in a room. Outer switches are three-way and the middle switch is a four-way. Requires two three-way switches and one four-way switch and two-wire and three-wire cables.

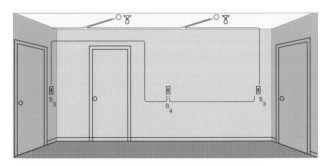

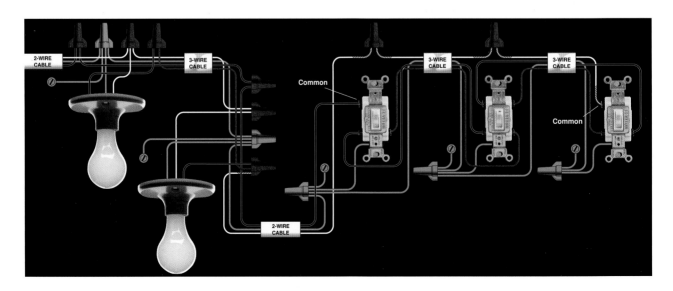

30. CEILING FAN/LIGHT FIXTURE CONTROLLED BY GANGED SWITCHES (FAN AT END OF CABLE RUN)

This layout is for a combination ceiling fan/light fixture controlled by a speed-control switch and dimmer in a double-gang switch box. Requires two-wire and three-wire cables.

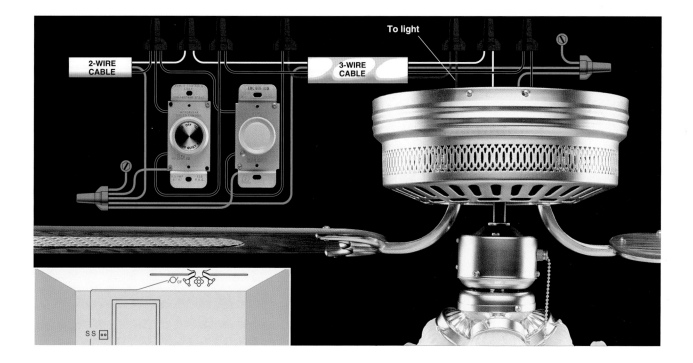

31. CEILING FAN/LIGHT FIXTURE CONTROLLED BY GANGED SWITCHES (SWITCHES AT END OF CABLE RUN)

Use this switch loop layout variation when it is more practical to install the ganged speed control and dimmer switches for the ceiling fan at the end of the cable run. Requires two-wire and three-wire cables.

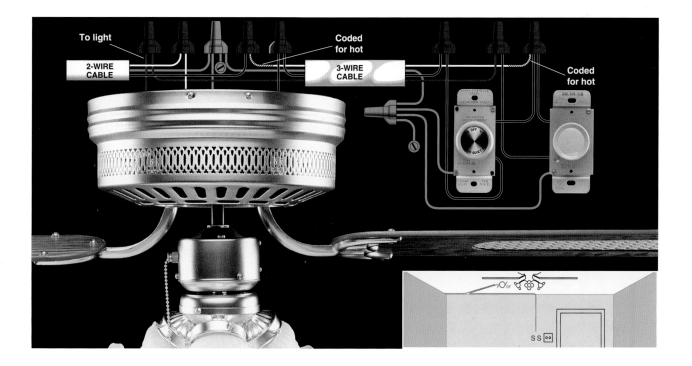

Panel Projects

Every home has a main service panel that distributes electrical current to the individual circuits. The main service panel usually is found in the basement, garage, or utility area, and can be identified by its metal casing. Before making any repair to your electrical system, you must shut off power to the correct circuit at the main service panel. The service panel should be indexed so circuits can be identified easily.

Service panels vary in appearance, depending on the age of the system. Very old wiring may operate on 30-amp service that has only two circuits. New homes can have 200-amp service with 30 or more circuits. Find the size of the service by reading the amperage rating printed on the main fuse block or main circuit breaker.

Regardless of age, all service panels have fuses or circuit breakers (page 8) that control each circuit and protect them from overloads. In general, older service panels use fuses, while newer service panels use circuit breakers.

In addition to the main service panel, your electrical system may have a subpanel that controls some of the circuits in the home. A subpanel has its own circuit breakers or fuses and is installed to control circuits that have been added to an existing wiring system.

The subpanel resembles the main service panel but is usually smaller. It may be located near the main panel, or it may be found near the areas served by the new circuits. Garages and basements that have been updated often have their own subpanels. If your home has a subpanel, make sure that its circuits are indexed correctly.

When handling fuses or circuit breakers, make sure the area around the service panel is dry. Never remove the protective cover on the service panel. After turning off a circuit to make electrical repairs, remember to always test the circuit for power before touching any wires.

Circuit Breaker Panels

The circuit breaker panel is the electrical distribution center for your home. It divides the current into branch circuits that are carried throughout the house. Each branch circuit is controlled by a circuit breaker that protects the wires from dangerous current overloads. When installing new circuits, the last step is to connect the wires to new circuit breakers at the panel. Working inside a circuit breaker panel is not dangerous if you follow basic safety procedures. Always shut off the main circuit breaker and test for power before touching any parts inside the panel, and never touch the service wire lugs. If unsure of your own skills, hire an electrician to make the final circuit connections. (If you have an older electrical service with fuses instead of circuit breakers, always have an electrician make these final hookups.)

If the main circuit breaker panel does not have enough open slots to hold new circuit breakers, install a subpanel (pages 40 to 44). This job is well within the skill level of an experienced do-it-yourselfer,

Slimline circuit breakers require half as much space as standard single-pole breakers. Slimlines can be used to make room for added circuits.

Grounding bus bar has terminals for linking grounding wires to the main grounding conductor. It is bonded to the neutral bus bar.

Main circuit breaker panel distributes the power entering the home into branch circuits.

Neutral service wire carries current back to the power source after it has passed through the home.

Two hot service wires provide 120 volts of power to the main circuit breaker. These wires are always HOT.

Main circuit breaker protects the hot service wires from overloads and transfers power to two hot bus bars.

Double-pole breaker wired for a 120/240 circuit transfers power from the two hot bus bars to red and black hot wires in a three-wire cable.

Neutral bus bar has setscrew terminals for linking all neutral circuit wires to the neutral service wire.

Service wire lugs: DO NOT TOUCH

120-volt branch circuits

Subpanel feeder breaker is a double-pole breaker, usually 30 to 50 amps. It is wired in the same way as a 120/240-volt circuit.

Two hot bus bars run through the center of the panel, supplying power to the circuit breakers. Each carries 120 volts.

Grounding conductor leads to metal grounding rods driven into the earth.

120/240-volt branch circuit

although you can also hire an electrician to install the subpanel.

Before installing any new wiring, evaluate your electrical service to make sure it provides enough current to support both the existing wiring and any new circuits. If your service does not provide enough power, have an electrician upgrade it to a higher amp rating. During the upgrade, the electrician will install a new circuit breaker panel with enough extra breaker slots for the new circuits you want to install.

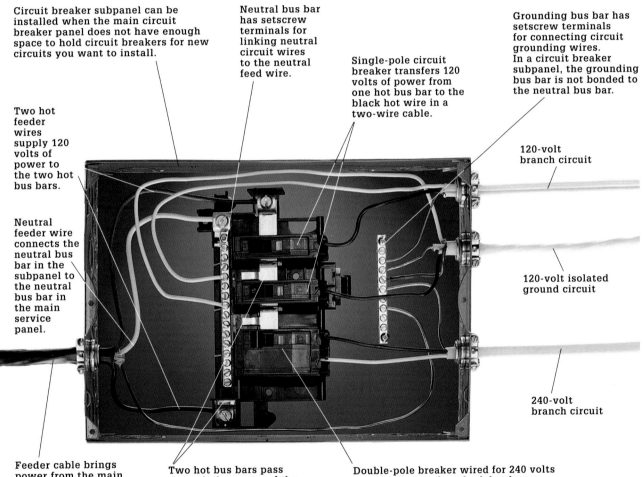

Circuit breaker subpanel can be installed when the main circuit breaker panel does not have enough space to hold circuit breakers for new circuits you want to install.

Neutral bus bar has setscrew terminals for linking neutral circuit wires to the neutral feed wire.

Single-pole circuit breaker transfers 120 volts of power from one hot bus bar to the black hot wire in a two-wire cable.

Grounding bus bar has setscrew terminals for connecting circuit grounding wires. In a circuit breaker subpanel, the grounding bus bar is not bonded to the neutral bus bar.

120-volt branch circuit

Two hot feeder wires supply 120 volts of power to the two hot bus bars.

120-volt isolated ground circuit

Neutral feeder wire connects the neutral bus bar in the subpanel to the neutral bus bar in the main service panel.

240-volt branch circuit

Feeder cable brings power from the main circuit breaker panel. A 30-amp, 240-volt subpanel requires a 10/3 feeder cable controlled by a 30-amp double-pole circuit breaker.

Two hot bus bars pass through the center of the service panel, supplying power to the individual circuit breakers. Each carries 120 volts of power.

Double-pole breaker wired for 240 volts transfers power from both hot bus bars to white and black hot wires in a two-wire cable. A 240-volt circuit has no neutral wire connection; the white wire is tagged with black tape to identify it as a hot wire.

Connecting Circuit Breakers

The last step in a wiring project is connecting circuits at the breaker panel. After this is done, the work is ready for the final inspection.

Circuits are connected at the main breaker panel, if it has enough open slots, or at a circuit breaker subpanel (pages 40 to 44). When working at a subpanel, make sure the feeder breaker at the main panel has been turned off, and test for power (photo, right) before touching any parts in the subpanel.

Make sure the circuit breaker amperage does not exceed the ampacity of the circuit wires you are connecting to it. Also be aware that circuit breaker styles and installation techniques vary according to manufacturer. Use breakers designed for your type of panel.

Tools & Materials ▸

Screwdriver
Hammer
Pencil
Combination tool
Cable ripper

Circuit tester
Pliers
Cable clamps
Single- and double-pole
   circuit breakers

Test for current before touching any parts inside a circuit breaker panel. With main breaker turned off but all other breakers turned on, touch one probe of a neon tester to the neutral bus bar, and touch other probe to each setscrew on one of the double-pole breakers (not the main breaker). If tester does not light for either setscrew, it is safe to work in the panel.

How to Connect Circuit Breakers

Shut off the main circuit breaker in the main circuit breaker panel (if you are working in a subpanel, shut off the feeder breaker in the main panel). Remove the panel cover plate, taking care not to touch the parts inside the panel. Test for power (photo, top).

Open a knockout in the side of the circuit breaker panel using a screwdriver and hammer. Attach a cable clamp to the knockout.

Hold cable across the front of the panel near the knockout, and mark sheathing about ½" inside the edge of the panel. Strip the cable from marked line to end using a cable ripper. (There should be 18 to 24" of excess cable.) Insert the cable through the clamp and into the service panel, then tighten the clamp.

Bend the bare copper grounding wire around the inside edge of the panel to an open setscrew terminal on the grounding bus bar. Insert the wire into the opening on the bus bar, and tighten the setscrew. Fold excess wire around the inside edge of the panel.

For 120-volt circuits, bend the white circuit wire around the outside of the panel to an open setscrew terminal on the neutral bus bar. Clip away excess wire, then strip ½" of insulation from the wire using a combination tool. Insert the wire into the terminal opening, and tighten the setscrew.

Strip ½" of insulation from the end of the black circuit wire. Insert the wire into the setscrew terminal on a new single-pole circuit breaker, and tighten the setscrew.

Slide one end of the circuit breaker onto the guide hook, then press it firmly against the bus bar until it snaps into place. (Breaker installation may vary, depending on the manufacturer.) Fold excess black wire around the inside edge of the panel.

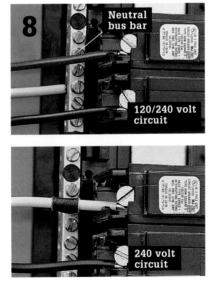

120/240-volt circuits (top): Connect red and black wires to double-pole breaker. Connect white wire to neutral bus bar, and grounding wire to grounding bus bar. For 240-volt circuits (bottom), attach white and black wires to double-pole breaker, tagging white wire with black tape. There is no neutral bus bar connection on this circuit.

Remove the appropriate breaker knockout on the panel cover plate to make room for the new circuit breaker. A single-pole breaker requires one knockout, while a double-pole breaker requires two knockouts. Reattach the cover plate, and label the new circuit on the panel index.

Installing a Subpanel

Install a circuit breaker subpanel if the main circuit breaker panel does not have enough open breaker slots for the new circuits you are planning. Called non-service rated panels in most code books, the subpanel serves as a second distribution center for connecting circuits. It receives power from a double-pole feeder circuit breaker you install in the main circuit breaker panel.

If the main service panel is so full that there is no room for the double-pole subpanel feeder breaker, you can reconnect some of the existing 120-volt circuits to special slimline breakers (photos below).

Plan your subpanel installation carefully, making sure your electrical service supplies enough power to support the extra load of the new subpanel circuits. Assuming your main service is adequate, consider installing an oversized subpanel feeder breaker in the main panel to provide enough extra amps to meet the needs of future wiring projects.

Also consider the physical size of the subpanel, and choose one that has enough extra slots to hold circuits you may want to install later. The smallest panels have room for up to six single-pole breakers

(or three double-pole breakers), while the largest models can hold up to 20 single-pole breakers.

Subpanels often are mounted near the main circuit breaker panel. Or, for convenience, they can be installed close to the areas they serve, such as in a new room addition or a garage. In a finished room, a subpanel can be painted or housed in a decorative cabinet so it is less of a visual distraction. If it is covered, make sure the subpanel is easily accessible and clearly identified.

Tools & Materials ▸

Hammer	Cable clamps
Screwdriver	Three-wire NM cable
Circuit tester	Cable staples
Cable ripper	Double-pole circuit breaker
Combination tool	Circuit breaker subpanel
Screws	Slimline circuit breakers

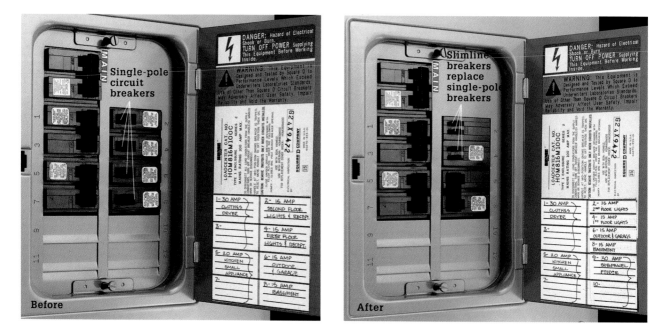

To conserve space in a service panel, you can replace single-pole breakers with slimline breakers. Slimline breakers take up half the space of standard breakers, allowing you to fit two circuits into one single slot on the service panel. In the service panel shown above, four single-pole 120-volt breakers were replaced with slimline breakers to provide the double opening needed for a 30-amp, 240-volt subpanel feeder breaker. Use slimline breakers with the same amp rating as the standard single-pole breakers you are removing, and make sure they are approved for use in your panel.

How to Plan a Subpanel Installation

1. Find the gross electrical load for only those areas that will be served by the subpanel. Refer to Evaluate Electrical Loads (pages 12 to 13). Example: In the 400-sq.-ft. attic room addition shown on pages 80 to 89, the gross load required for the basic lighting/receptacle circuits and electric heating is 5,000 watts.	Gross electrical load:	_5,000_ watts
2. Multiply the gross electrical load times 1.25. This safety adjustment is required by the National Electrical Code. Example: In the attic room addition (gross load 5,000 watts), the adjusted load equals 6,250 watts.	_5,000_ watts × 1.25 =	_6,250_ watts
3. Convert the load into amps by dividing by 230. This gives the required amperage needed to power the subpanel. Example: The attic room addition described above requires about 27 amps of power (6,250 ÷ 230).	_6,250_ watts ÷ 230 =	_27.2_ amps
4. For the subpanel feeder breaker, choose a double-pole circuit breaker with an amp rating equal to or greater than the required subpanel amperage. Example: In a room addition that requires 27 amps, choose a 30-amp double-pole feeder breaker.	☒ 30-amp breaker ☐ 40-amp breaker ☐ 50-amp breaker	
5. For the feeder cable bringing power from the main circuit breaker panel to the subpanel, choose three-wire NM cable with an ampacity equal to the rating of the subpanel feeder breaker. Example: For a 40-amp subpanel feeder breaker, choose 8/3 cable for the feeder.	☐ 10/3 cable ☒ 8/3 cable ☐ 6/3 cable	

How to Install a Subpanel

Mount the subpanel at shoulder height following manufacturer's recommendations. The subpanel can be mounted to the sides of studs or to plywood attached between two studs. Panel shown here extends ½" past the face of studs so it will be flush with the finished wall surface.

Open a knockout in the subpanel using a screwdriver and hammer. Run the feeder cable from the main circuit breaker panel to the subpanel, leaving about 2 ft. of excess cable at each end. See page 59 if you need to run the cable through finished walls.

Attach a cable clamp to the knockout in the subpanel. Insert the cable into the subpanel, then anchor it to framing members within 8" of each panel, and every 4 ft. thereafter.

(continued)

Strip away outer sheathing from the feeder cable using a cable ripper. Leave at least ¼" of sheathing extending into the subpanel. Tighten the cable clamp screws so cable is held securely, but not so tightly that the wire sheathing is crushed.

Strip ½" of insulation from the white neutral feeder wire, and attach it to the main lug on the subpanel neutral bus bar. Connect the grounding wire to a setscrew terminal on the grounding bus bar. Fold excess wire around the inside edge of the subpanel.

Strip away ½" of insulation from the red and the black feeder wires. Attach one wire to the main lug on each of the hot bus bars. Fold excess wire around the inside edge of the subpanel.

At the main circuit breaker panel, shut off the main circuit breaker, then remove the coverplate and test for power. If necessary, make room for the double-pole feeder breaker by removing single-pole breakers and reconnecting the wires to slimline circuit breakers. Open a knockout for the feeder cable using a hammer and screwdriver.

Strip away the outer sheathing from the feeder cable so that at least ¼" of sheathing will reach into the main service panel. Attach a cable clamp to the cable, then insert the cable into the knockout, and anchor it by threading a locknut onto the clamp. Tighten the locknut by driving a screwdriver against the lugs. Tighten the clamp screws so the cable is held securely, but not so tightly that the cable sheathing is crushed.

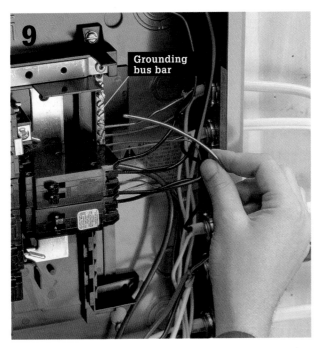

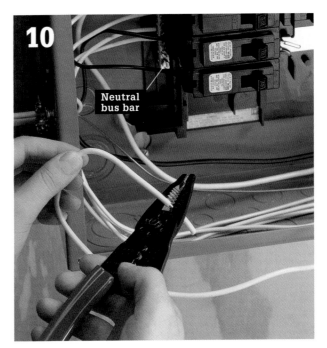

Bend the bare copper wire from the feeder cable around the inside edge of the main circuit breaker panel, and connect it to one of the setscrew terminals on the grounding bus bar.

Strip away ½" of insulation from the white feeder wire. Attach the wire to one of the setscrew terminals on the neutral bus bar. Fold excess wire around the inside edge of the service panel.

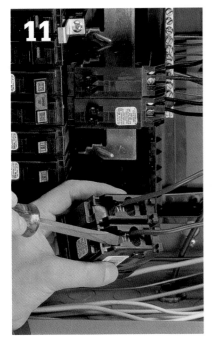

Strip ½" of insulation from the red and the black feeder wires. Attach one wire to each of the setscrew terminals on the double-pole feeder breaker.

Hook the end of the feeder circuit breaker over the guide hooks on the panel, then push the other end forward until the breaker snaps onto the hot bus bars (follow manufacturer's directions). Fold excess wire around the inside edge of the circuit breaker panel.

If necessary, open two knockouts where the double-pole feeder breaker will fit, then reattach the cover plate. Label the feeder breaker on the circuit index. Turn main breaker on, but leave feeder breaker off until all subpanel circuits have been connected and inspected.

Upgrading a Service Panel

Only a generation ago, fuse boxes were commonplace. But as our demands for power increased, homeowners replaced the 60-amp boxes with larger, safer, and more reliable circuit breaker panels. Typical new homes were built with perfectly adequate 100-amp load centers. But today, as average home size has risen to more than 2,500 sg. ft. and the number of home electronics has risen exponentially, 100 amps is only adequate service. As a result, many homeowners have upgraded to 200-amp service, and new single-family homes often include 250-amps or even 300-amps of power.

Upgrading your electrical service panel from 100 amps to 200 amps is an ambitious project that requires a lot of forethought. To do the job, you will need to have your utility company disconnect your house from electrical service at the transformer that feeds your house. Not only does this involve working them into your schedule, it means you will have no power during the project. You can rent a portable generator to provide a circuit or two, or you can run a couple extension cords from a friendly neighbor. But unless you are a very fast worker, plan on being without power for at least a day while the project is in process.

Also check with your utility company to make sure you know what equipment is theirs and what belongs to you. In most cases, the electric meter and everything on the street side belongs to the power company, and the meter base and everything on the house side is yours. Be aware that if you tamper with the sealed meter in any way, you likely will be fined.

Upgrading a service panel is a major project. Do not hesitate to call for help at any point if you're unsure what to do.

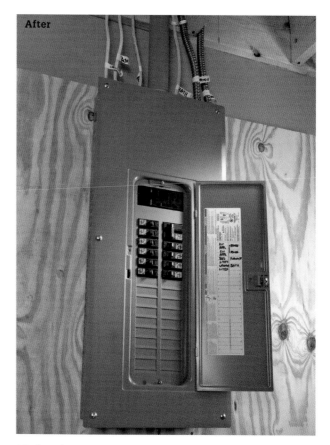

Modern homeowners consume more power than our forebears, and it is often necessary to upgrade the electrical service to keep pace. While homeowners are not allowed to make the final electrical service connections, removing the old panel and installing the new panel and meter base yourself can save you hundreds or even thousands of dollars.

Tools & Materials ▸

200-amp load center (service panel)
200-amp bypass meter base
Circuit breakers
Schedule 80 or IMC conduit and fittings
Weatherhead
Service entry cable
Circuit wires
Plywood backer board
Screwdrivers
Drill/driver
Tape
Allen wrench
Circuit tester
Multimeter

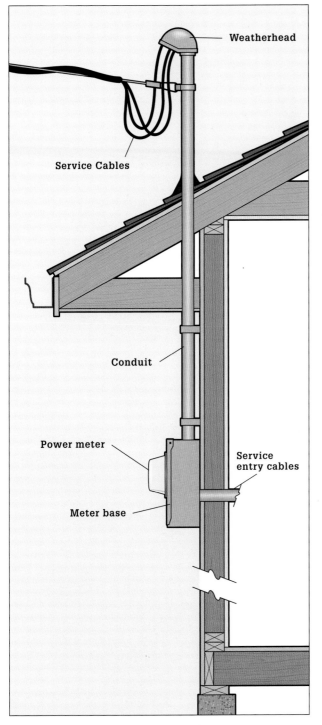

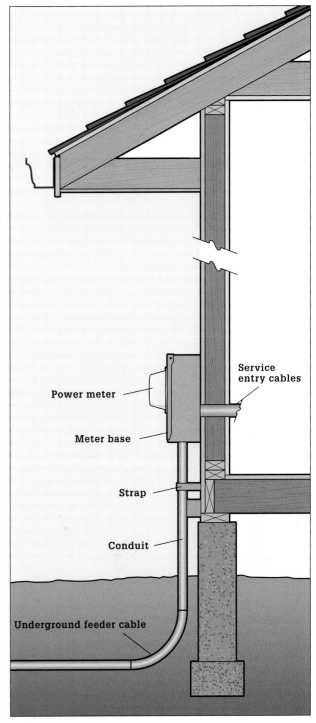

Aboveground meter with riser. In this common configuration, the power cables from the closest transformer (called the service drop) are connected to the power distribution system in your house inside a protective hood called a weatherhead. The service cables from the weatherhead are routed to a power meter that's owned by your utility company but is housed in a base that's considered your property. From the meter the cables (called service entry cables or SECs) enter your house through the wall and are routed to the main service panel, where they are connected to the main circuit breaker.

Underground service feeder. Increasingly, homebuilders are choosing to have power supplied to their new homes through underground feeder cable instead of an overhead service drop. Running the cables in the ground eliminates problems with power outages caused by ice accumulation or fallen trees, but it entails a completely different set of cable and conduit requirements. For the homeowner, however, the differences are minimal because the hookups are identical once the power service reaches the meter.

Locating Your New Panel ▸

Local codes dictate where the main service panel may be placed relative to other parts of your home. Although the codes may vary (and always take precedence), national codes stipulate that a service panel (or any other distribution panel) may not be located near flammable materials, in a bathroom, in an area with a ceiling height less than 78", or directly above a workbench or other permanent work station or appliance. The panel also can't be located in a crawl space or in a partial basement. The panel must be framed with at least 30" of clear space on all sides. If you are installing a new service entry hookup, there are many regulations regarding height of the service drop and the meter (the meter should always be located 66" above grade). Contact your local inspections office for specific regulations.

All the equipment you'll need to upgrade your main panel is sold at most larger building centers. It includes (A) a new 200-amp panel; (B) a 200-amp bypass meter base (also called a socket); (C) individual circuit breakers (if your new panel is the same brand as your old one you may be able to reuse the old breakers); (D) new, usually larger, SE cable (2/0 copper seen here); (E) 2" dia. rigid conduit; (F) weatherhead shroud for mast.

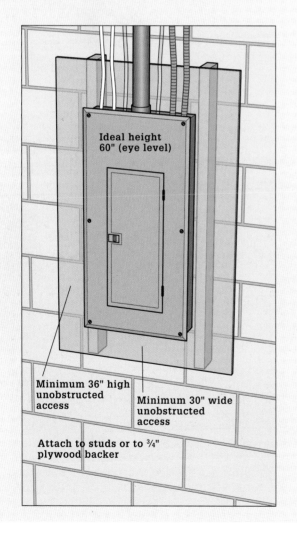

Ideal height 60" (eye level)

Minimum 36" high unobstructed access

Minimum 30" wide unobstructed access

Attach to studs or to ¾" plywood backer

Meter

Shutoff switch

A shutoff switch next to the electric meter is required if your main service panel is too far away from the point where the service cable enters your house. The maximum distance allowed varies widely, from as little as 3 ft. to more than 10 ft. Wiring the service cable through the shutoff has the effect of transforming your main service panel into a subpanel, which will impact how the neutral and ground wires are attached (see Subpanels, pages 40 to 44).

How to Replace a Main Service Panel

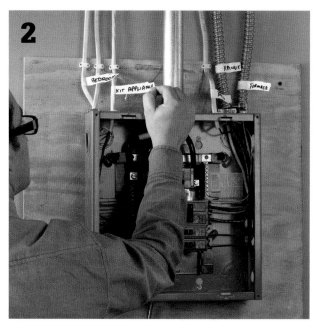

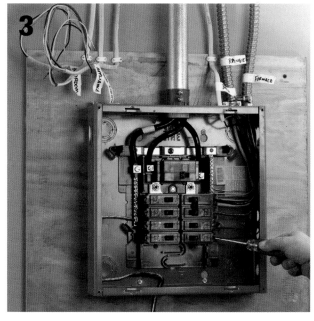

Shut off power to the house at the transformer. This must be done by a technician who is certified by your utility company. Also have the utility worker remove the old meter from the base. It is against the law for a homeowner to break the seal on the meter.

Label all incoming circuit wires before disconnecting them. Labels should be written clearly on tape that is attached to the cables outside of the existing service panel.

Disconnect incoming circuit wires from breakers, grounding bar, and neutral bus bar. Also disconnect cable clamps at the knockouts on the panel box. Retract all circuit wires from the service panel and coil up neatly, with the labels clearly visible.

Unscrew the lugs securing the service entry cables at the top of the panel. For 240-volt service you will find two heavy-gauge SE cables, probably with black sheathing. Each cable carries 120 volts of electricity. A neutral service cable, usually of lighter gauge than the SE cables, will be attached to the neutral bus bar. This cable returns current to the source.

(continued)

5

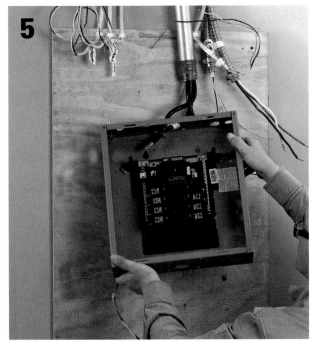

Remove the old service panel box. Boxes are rated for a range of power service; and if you are upgrading, the components in the old box will be undersized for the new service levels. The new box will have a greater number of circuit slots as well.

6

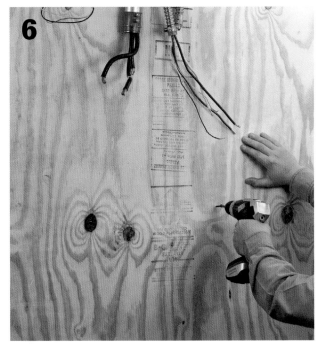

Replace the old panel backer board with a larger board in the installation area (see sidebar, page 46). A piece of ¾" plywood is typical. Make sure the board is well secured at wall framing members.

7

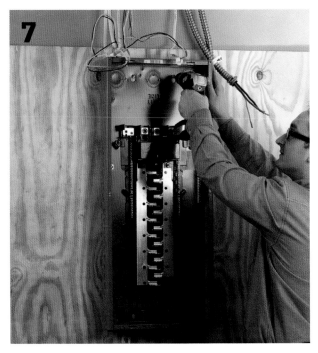

Attach the new service panel box to the backer board, making sure that at least two screws are driven through the backer and into wall studs. Drill clearance holes in the back of the box at stud locations if necessary. Use roundhead screws that do not have tapered shanks so the screwhead seats flat against the panel.

8

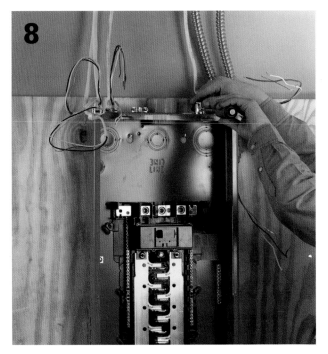

Attach properly sized cable clamps to the box at the knockout holes. Do not crowd multiple lines into a knockout hole, and plan carefully to avoid removing knockouts that you do not need to remove (if you do make a mistake, you can fill the knockout hole with a plug).

Tip ▶

Some wiring codes allow you to make splices inside the service panel box if the circuit wire is too short. Use the correct wire connector and wind electrical tape over the conductors where they enter the cap. If your municipality does not allow splices in the panel box, you'll have to rectify a short cable by splicing it in a junction box before it reaches the panel, and then replacing the cable with a longer section for the end of the run. Make sure each circuit line has at least 12" of slack.

Attach the white neutral from each circuit cable to the neutral bus bar. Most panels have a preinstalled neutral bus bar, but in some cases you may need to purchase the bar separately and attach it to the panel back. The panel should also have a separate grounding bar that you also may need to purchase separately. Attach the grounds as well (it's generally allowed to twist bare ground wires together and attach them to a single screw terminal). Do not attach neutrals and grounding wires to the same bar.

Attach the hot lead wire to the terminal on the circuit breaker and then snap the breaker into an empty slot. When loading slots, start at the top of the panel and work your way downward. It is important that you balance the circuits as you go to equalize the amperage. For example, do not install all the 15 amp circuits on one side and all the 20 amp circuits on the other. Also, if you have multiple larger-capacity circuits, such as a 50-amp dryer and a 50-amp range, do not install them on the same side of the panel in case they will be drawing electricity at the same time.

Create an accurate circuit index and affix it to the inside of the service panel door. List all loads that are on the circuit as well as the amperage. Once you have restored power to the new service panel (see step 18), test out each circuit to make sure you don't have any surprises. With the main breakers on, shut off all individual circuit breakers and then flip each one on by itself. Walk through your house and test every switch and receptacle to confirm the loads on that circuit.

(continued)

Install grounding conductors. Local codes are very specific about how the grounding needs to be accomplished. For example, some require multiple rods driven at least 6 ft. apart. Discuss your grounding requirements thoroughly with your inspector or an electrician before making your plan.

Replace the old meter base (have the utility company remove the meter when they shut off power to the house, step 1). Remove the old meter base, also called a socket, and install a new base that's rated for the amperage of your new power service. Here, a 200-amp bypass meter base is being installed.

Update the conduit that runs from your house to the bottom of the meter base. This should be 2" rigid conduit in good repair. Attach the conduit to the base and wall with the correct fittings.

Install new service entry wires. Each wire carries 120 volts of current from the meter to the service wire lugs at the top of your service panel. Code is very specific about how these connections are made. In most cases, you'll need to tighten the terminal nuts with a specific amount of torque that requires a torque wrench to measure. Also attach the sheathed neutral wire to the neutral/grounding lug.

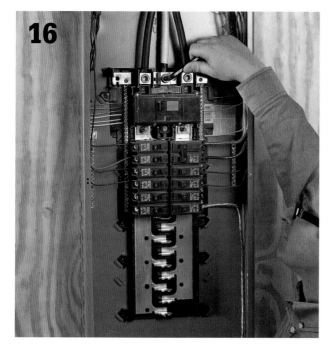

16

Attach the SE wires to the lugs connected to the main breakers at the top of your service entry panel. Do not remove too much insulation on the wires—leaving the wires exposed is a safety hazard. The neutral service entry wire is attached either directly to the neutral bus bar or to a metal bridge that is connected to the neutral bonding bus bar.

17

Install service entry wires from the meter to the weatherhead, where the connections to the power source are made. Only an agent for your public utility company may make the hookup at the weatherhead.

Tip ▶

The service drop must occur at least 10 ft. above ground level, and as much as 14 ft. in some cases. Occasionally, this means that you must run the conduit for the service mast up through the eave of your roof and seal the roof penetration with a boot.

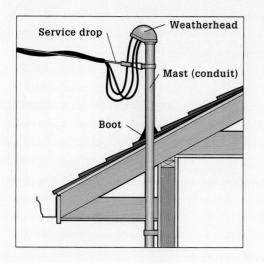

Service drop — Weatherhead

Mast (conduit)

Boot

18

Have the panel and all connections inspected and approved by your local building department, and then contact the public utility company to make the connections at the power drop. Once the connections are made, turn the main breakers on and test all circuits.

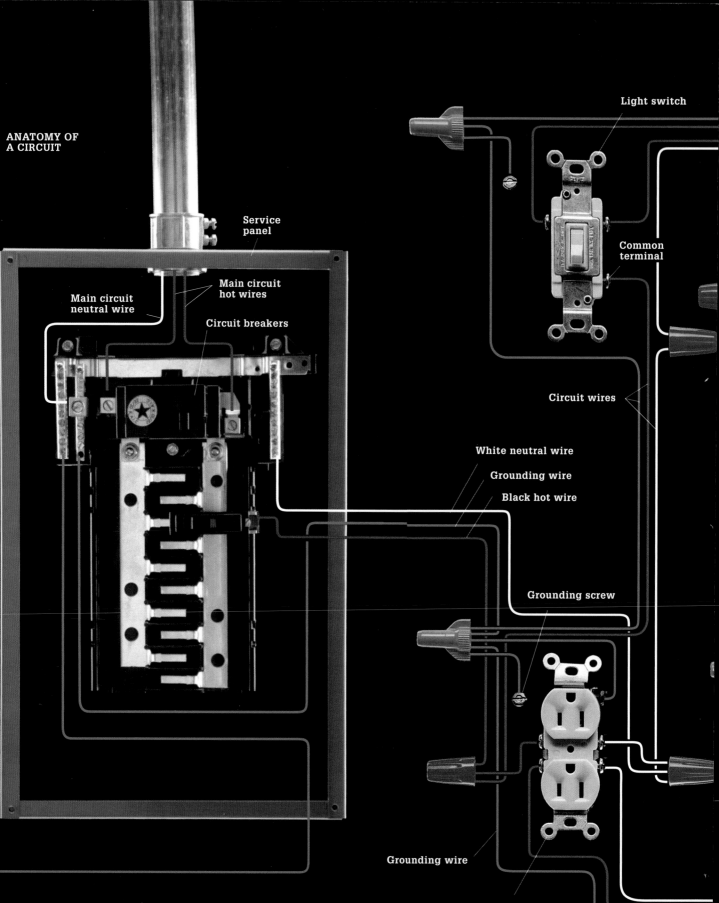

ANATOMY OF
A CIRCUIT

Service
panel

Main circuit
hot wires

Main circuit
neutral wire

Circuit breakers

Light switch

Common
terminal

Circuit wires

White neutral wire

Grounding wire

Black hot wire

Grounding screw

Grounding wire

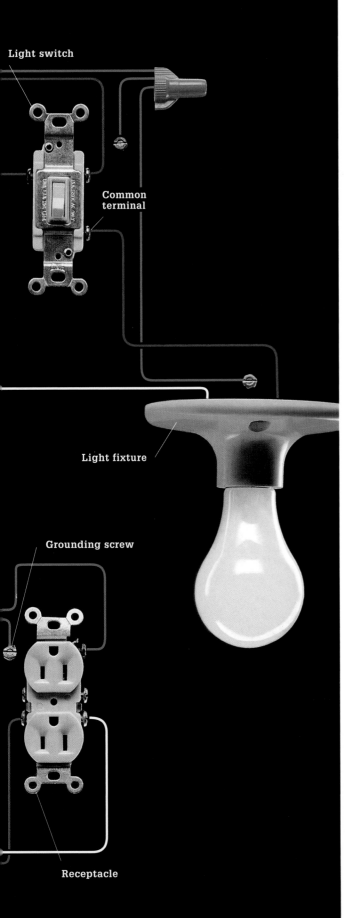

Light switch

Common terminal

Light fixture

Grounding screw

Receptacle

Adding Circuits

An electrical circuit is a continuous loop. Household circuits carry power from the main service panel, throughout the house, and back to the main service panel. Several switches, receptacles, light fixtures, or appliances may be connected to a single circuit.

Current enters a circuit loop on hot wires and returns along neutral wires. These wires are color coded for easy identification. Hot wires are black or red, and neutral wires are white or light gray. For safety, most circuits include a bare copper or green insulated grounding wire. The grounding wire conducts current in the event of a short circuit or overload, and helps reduce the chance of severe electrical shock. The service panel also has a grounding wire connected to a metal water pipe and metal grounding rod buried underground.

If a circuit carries too much power, it can overload. A fuse or a circuit breaker protects each circuit in case of overloads.

Current returns to the service panel along a neutral circuit wire. Current then becomes part of a main circuit and leaves the house on a large neutral service wire that returns it to the utility pole transformer.

Running New Cable

Non-metallic (NM) cable is used for all indoor wiring projects except those requiring conduit. Cut and install the cable after all electrical boxes have been mounted. Refer to your wiring plan to make sure each length of cable is correct for the circuit size and configuration.

Cable runs are difficult to measure exactly, so leave plenty of extra wire when cutting each length. Cable splices inside walls are not allowed by code. When inserting cables into a circuit breaker panel, make sure the power is shut off.

After all cables are installed, call your electrical inspector to arrange for the rough-in inspection. Do not install wallboard or attach light fixtures and other devices until this inspection is done.

Tools & Materials ▸

Drill
Bits
Tape measure
Cable ripper
Combination tool
Screwdrivers
Needlenose pliers
Hammer

Fish tape
NM cable
Cable clamps
Cable staples
Masking tape
Grounding pigtails
Wire connectors

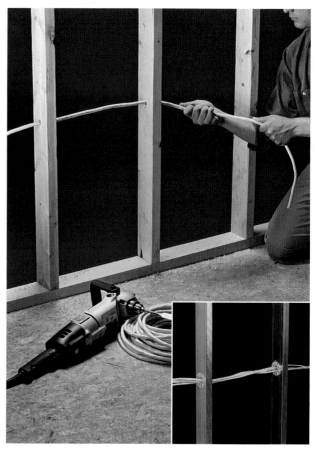

Pulling cables through studs is easier if you drill smooth, straight holes at the same height. Prevent kinks by straightening the cable before pulling it through the studs. Use plastic grommets to protect cables on steel studs (inset).

Framing member	Maximum hole size	Maximum notch size
2 × 4 loadbearing stud	1⁷⁄₁₆" diameter	⁷⁄₈" deep
2 × 4 non-loadbearing stud	2½" diameter	1⁷⁄₁₆" deep
2 × 6 loadbearing stud	2¼" diameter	1⅜" deep
2 × 6 non-loadbearing stud	3⁵⁄₁₆" diameter	2³⁄₁₆" deep
2 × 6 joists	1½" diameter	⁷⁄₈" deep
2 × 8 joists	2⅜" diameter	1¼" deep
2 × 10 joists	3¹⁄₁₆" diameter	1½" deep
2 × 12 joists	3¾" diameter	1⅞" deep

This framing member chart shows the maximum sizes for holes and notches that can be cut into studs and joists when running cables. When boring holes, there must be at least 1¼" of wood between the edge of a stud and the hole, and at least 2" between the edge of a joist and the hole. Joists can be notched only in the end ⅓ of the overall span; never in the middle ⅓ of the joist.

How to Install NM Cable

Drill ⅝" holes in framing members for the cable runs. This is done easily with a right-angle drill, available at rental centers. Holes should be set back at least 1¼" from the front face of the framing members.

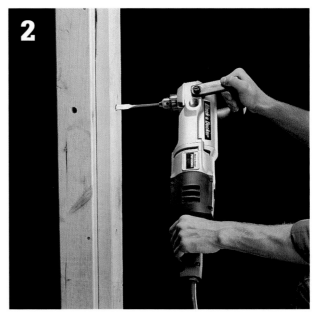

Where cables will turn corners (step 6, page 56), drill intersecting holes in adjoining faces of studs. Measure and cut all cables, allowing 2 ft. extra at ends entering the breaker panel and 1 foot for ends entering the electrical box.

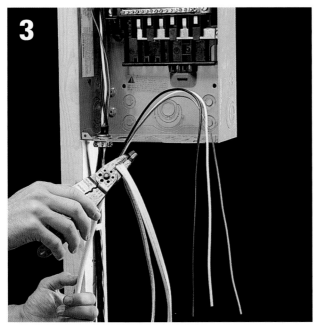

Shut off power to circuit breaker panel. Use a cable ripper to strip cable, leaving at least ¼" of sheathing to enter the circuit breaker panel. Clip away the excess sheathing.

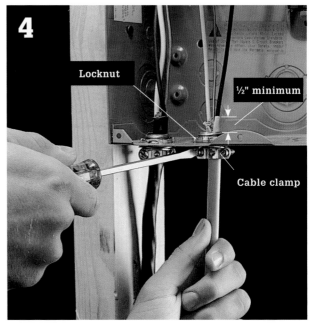

Locknut

½" minimum

Cable clamp

Open a knockout in the circuit breaker panel using a hammer and screwdriver. Insert a cable clamp into the knockout, and secure it with a locknut. Insert the cable through the clamp so that at least ½" of sheathing extends inside the circuit breaker panel. Tighten the mounting screws on the clamp so the cable is gripped securely but not so tightly that the sheathing is crushed.

(continued)

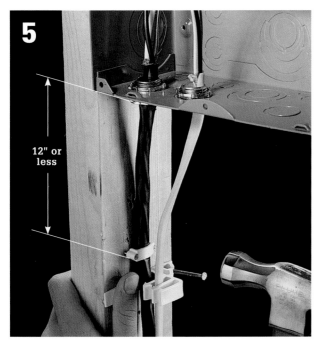

5

12" or less

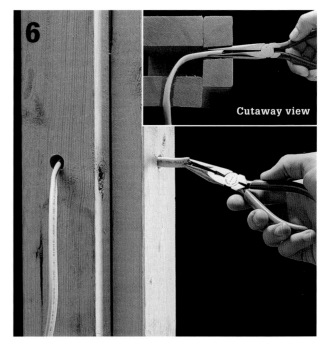

6

Cutaway view

Anchor the cable to the center of a framing member within 12" of the circuit breaker panel using a cable staple. Stack-It® staples work well where two or more cables must be anchored to the same side of a stud. Run the cable to the first electrical box. Where the cable runs along the sides of framing members, anchor it with cable staples no more than 4 ft. apart.

At corners, form a slight L-shaped bend in the end of the cable and insert it into one hole. Retrieve the cable through the other hole using needlenose pliers (inset).

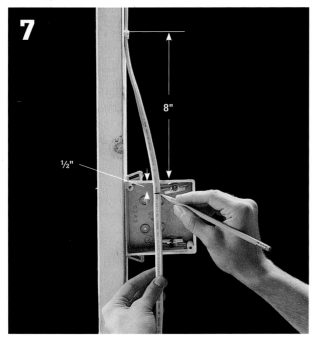

7

8"

½"

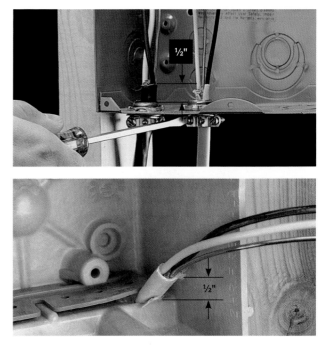

½"

½"

Staple the cable to a framing member 8" from the box. Hold the cable taut against the front of the box, and mark a point on the sheathing ½" past the box edge. Remove sheathing from the marked line to the end using a cable ripper, and clip away excess sheathing with a combination tool. Insert the cable through the knockout in the box.

Variation: Different types of boxes have different clamping devices. Make sure cable sheathing extends ½" past the edge of the clamp to ensure that the cable is secure and that the wire won't be damaged by the edges of the clamp.

8

As each cable is installed in a box, clip back each wire so that 8" of workable wire extends past the front edge of the box.

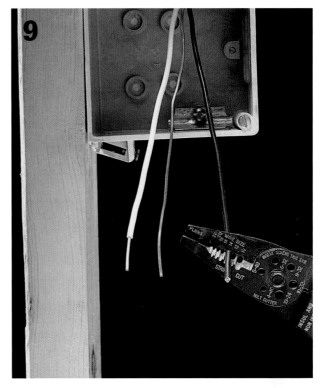

9

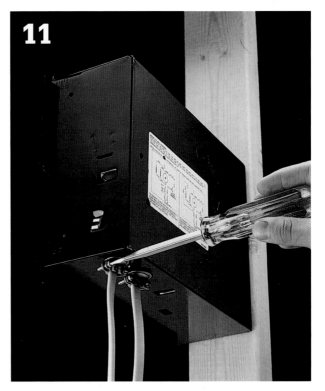

Strip ¾" of insulation from each circuit wire in the box using a combination tool. Take care not to nick the copper.

10

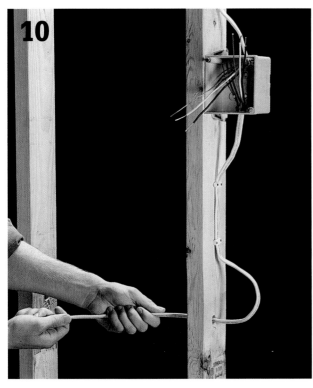

Continue the circuit by running cable between each pair of electrical boxes, leaving an extra 1 ft. of cable at each end.

11

At metal boxes and recessed fixtures, open knockouts, and attach cables with cable clamps. From inside fixture, strip away all but ¼" of sheathing. Clip back wires so there is 8" of workable length, then strip ¾" of insulation from each wire.

(continued)

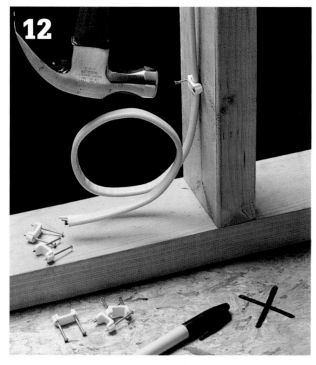

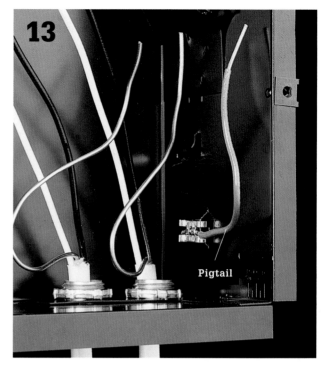

For a surface-mounted fixture like a baseboard heater or fluorescent light fixture, staple the cable to a stud near the fixture location, leaving plenty of excess cable. Mark the floor so the cable will be easy to find after the walls are finished.

At each recessed fixture and metal electrical box, connect one end of a grounding pigtail to the metal frame using a grounding clip attached to the frame (shown above) or a green grounding screw.

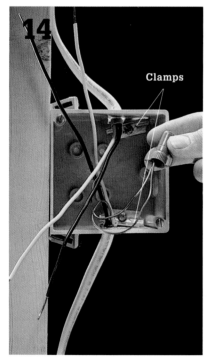

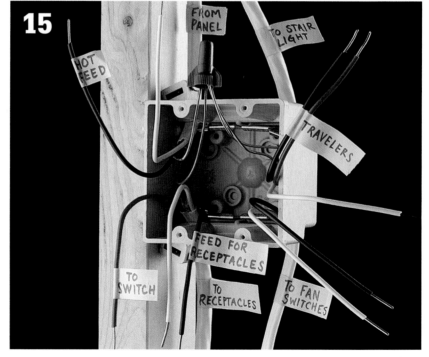

At each electrical box and recessed fixture, join grounding wires together with a wire connector. If the box has internal clamps, tighten the clamps over the cables.

Label the cables entering each box to indicate their destinations. In boxes with complex wiring configurations, also tag the individual wires to make final hookups easier. After all cables are installed, your rough-in work is ready to be reviewed by the electrical inspector.

How to Run NM Cable Inside a Finished Wall

From the unfinished space below the finished wall, look for a reference point, like a soil stack, plumbing pipes, or electrical cables, that indicates the location of the wall above. Choose a location for the new cable that does not interfere with existing utilities. Drill a 1" hole up into the stud cavity.

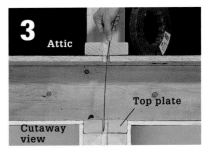
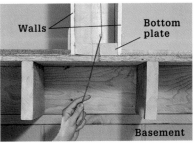

From the unfinished space above the finished wall, find the top of the stud cavity by measuring from the same fixed reference point used in step 1. Drill a 1" hole down through the top plate and into the stud cavity using a drill bit extender.

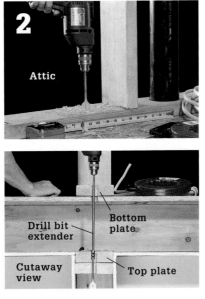

Extend a fish tape down through the top plate, twisting the tape until it reaches the bottom of the stud cavity. From the unfinished space below the wall, use a piece of stiff wire with a hook on one end to retrieve the fish tape through the drilled hole in the bottom plate.

Trim back 2" of sheathing from the end of the NM cable, then insert the wires through the loop at the tip of the fish tape.

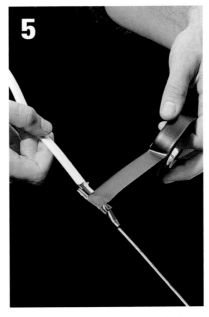

Bend the wires against the cable, then use electrical tape to bind them tightly. Apply cable-pulling lubricant to the taped end of the fish tape.

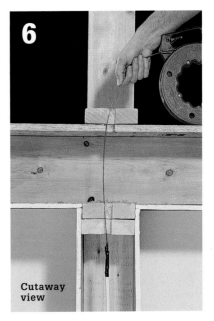

From above the finished wall, pull steadily on the fish tape to draw the cable up through the stud cavity. This job will be easier if you have a helper feed the cable from below as you pull.

Running Cable Inside Finished Walls

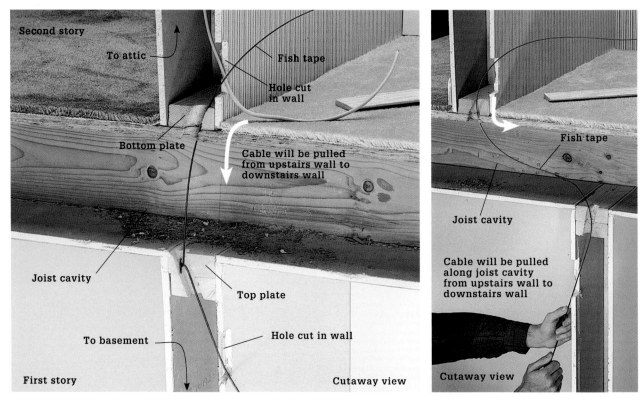

Second story
To attic
Fish tape
Hole cut in wall
Bottom plate
Cable will be pulled from upstairs wall to downstairs wall
Joist cavity
Top plate
To basement
Hole cut in wall
First story
Cutaway view

Fish tape
Joist cavity
Cable will be pulled along joist cavity from upstairs wall to downstairs wall
Cutaway view

If there is no access space above and below a wall, cut openings in the finished walls to run a cable. This often occurs in two-story homes when a cable is extended from an upstairs wall to a downstairs wall. Cut small openings in the wall near the top and bottom plates, then drill an angled 1" hole through each plate. Extend a fish tape into the joist cavity between the walls and use it to pull the cable from one wall to the next. If the walls line up one over the other (left), you can retrieve the fish tape using a piece of stiff wire. If walls do not line up (right), use a second fish tape. After running the cable, repair the holes in the walls with patching plaster or wallboard scraps and taping compound.

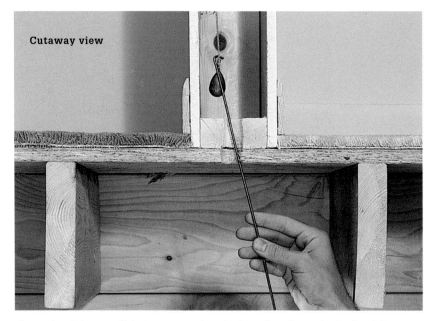

Cutaway view

If you don't have a fish tape, use a length of sturdy string and a lead weight or heavy washer. Drop the line into the stud cavity from above, then use a piece of stiff wire to hook the line from below.

Use a flexible drill bit, also called a bell-hanger's bit, to bore holes through framing in finished walls.

Installing NM Cable in Finished Ceilings

If you don't have access to a ceiling from above, you can run cable for a new ceiling fixture from an existing receptacle in the room up the wall and into the ceiling without disturbing much of the ceiling. To begin, run cable from the receptacle to the stud channel that aligns with the ceiling joists on which you want to install a fixture. Be sure to plan a location for the new switch. Remove short strips of drywall from the wall and ceiling. Make a notch in the center of the top plates, and protect the notch with metal nail stops. Use a fish tape to pull the new cable up through the wall cavity and the notch in top plates. Next, use the fish tape to pull the cable through the ceiling to the fixture hole. After having your work inspected, replace the drywall and install the fixture and switch.

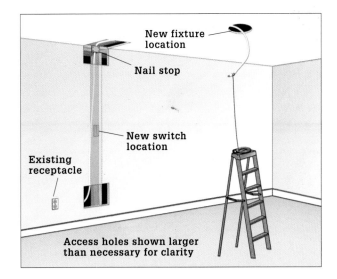

New fixture location

Nail stop

New switch location

Existing receptacle

Access holes shown larger than necessary for clarity

How to Install NM Cable in Finished Ceilings

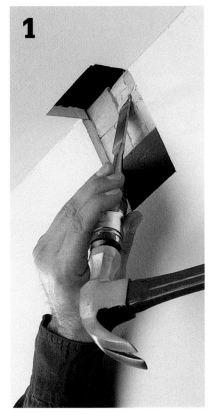

1

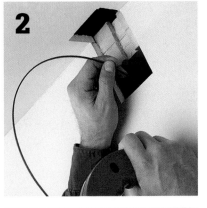

2

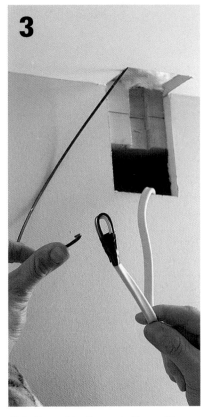

3

Plan a route for running cable between electrical boxes (see illustration above). Remove drywall on the wall and ceiling surface. Where cable must cross framing members, cut a small access opening in the wall and ceiling surface; then cut a notch into the framing with a wood chisel.

Fish a cable from the existing receptacle locationup to the notch at the top of the wall. Protect the notch with a metal nail stop. Fish the cable through the ceiling to the location of the new ceiling fixture.

Fish the cable through the ceiling to the location of the new ceiling fixture.

Installing Conduit

lectrical wiring that runs in exposed locations must be protected by rigid tubing called conduit. Thermoplastic high-heat-resistant-nylon-coated/ thermoplastic high-heat-resistant-nylon-coated-wet-locations (THHN/THWN) wire normally is installed inside conduit, although underground feeder (UF) or NM cable can also be installed in conduit.

There are several types of conduit available, so check with your electrical inspector to find out which type meets code requirements in your area. Conduit installed outdoors must be rated for exterior use. Metal conduit should be used only with metal boxes. At one time, conduit could only be fitted by using elaborate bending techniques and special tools. Now a variety of shaped fittings are available to let a homeowner easily join conduit.

Electrical Grounding in Metal Conduit

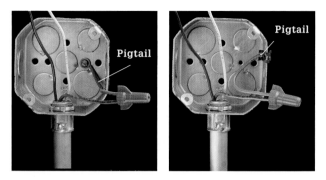

Install a green insulated grounding wire for any circuit that runs through metal conduit. Although code allows the metal conduit to serve as the grounding conductor, most electricians install a green insulated wire as a more dependable means of grounding the system. The grounding wires must be connected to metal boxes with a pigtail and grounding screw (left) or grounding clip (right).

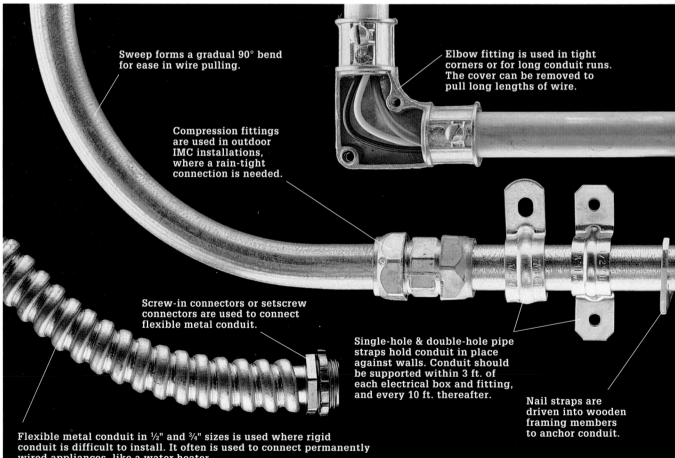

Sweep forms a gradual 90° bend for ease in wire pulling.

Elbow fitting is used in tight corners or for long conduit runs. The cover can be removed to pull long lengths of wire.

Compression fittings are used in outdoor IMC installations, where a rain-tight connection is needed.

Screw-in connectors or setscrew connectors are used to connect flexible metal conduit.

Single-hole & double-hole pipe straps hold conduit in place against walls. Conduit should be supported within 3 ft. of each electrical box and fitting, and every 10 ft. thereafter.

Nail straps are driven into wooden framing members to anchor conduit.

Flexible metal conduit in ½" and ¾" sizes is used where rigid conduit is difficult to install. It often is used to connect permanently wired appliances, like a water heater.

Fill Capacity

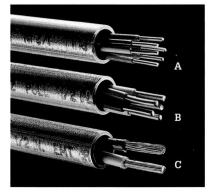

Conduit ½" in diameter can hold up to six 14-gauge or 12-gauge THHN/THWN wires (A), five 10-gauge wires (B), or two 8-gauge wires (C). Use ¾" conduit for greater capacity.

Metal Conduit

EMT (electrical metallic tubing)

IMC (intermediate metallic conduit)

Rigid metal conduit

EMT is lightweight and easy to install but should not be used where it can be damaged. IMC has thicker galvanized walls and is a good choice for exposed outdoor use. Rigid metal conduit provides the greatest protection for wires, but it is more expensive and requires threaded fittings.

Plastic Conduit

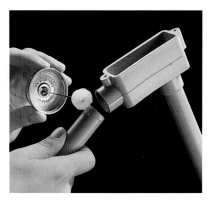

Plastic PVC conduit is allowed by many local codes. It is assembled with solvent glue and PVC fittings that resemble those for metal conduit. When wiring with PVC conduit, always run a green grounding wire.

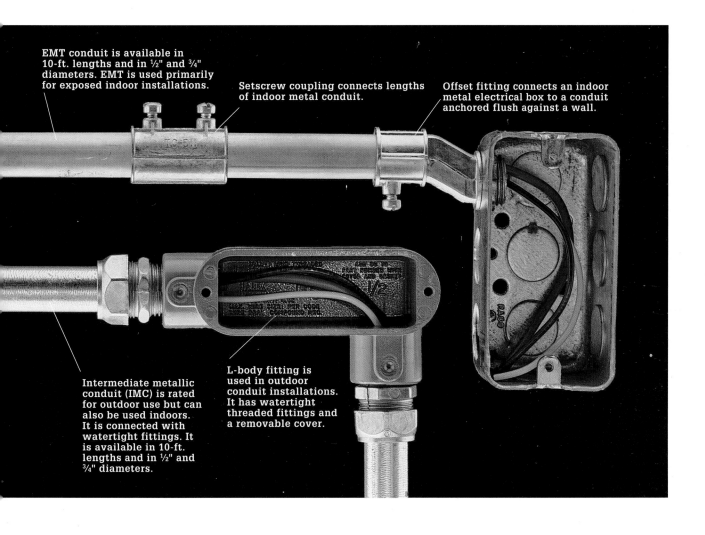

EMT conduit is available in 10-ft. lengths and in ½" and ¾" diameters. EMT is used primarily for exposed indoor installations.

Setscrew coupling connects lengths of indoor metal conduit.

Offset fitting connects an indoor metal electrical box to a conduit anchored flush against a wall.

Intermediate metallic conduit (IMC) is rated for outdoor use but can also be used indoors. It is connected with watertight fittings. It is available in 10-ft. lengths and in ½" and ¾" diameters.

L-body fitting is used in outdoor conduit installations. It has watertight threaded fittings and a removable cover.

Working with Conduit

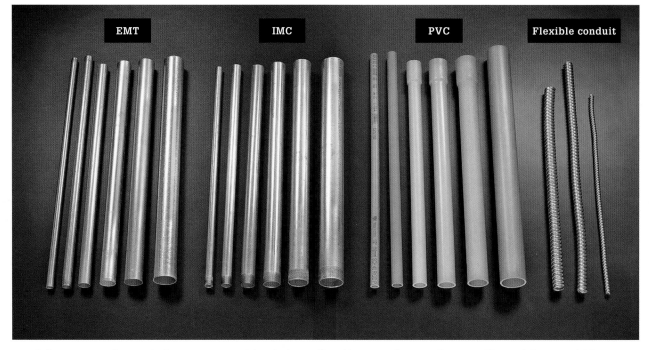

EMT | IMC | PVC | Flexible conduit

Conduit types used most in homes are EMT (electrical metallic tubing), IMC (intermediate metallic conduit), RNC (rigid nonmetallic conduit), and flexible metal conduit. The most common diameters by far are ½" and ¾", but larger sizes are stocked at most building centers.

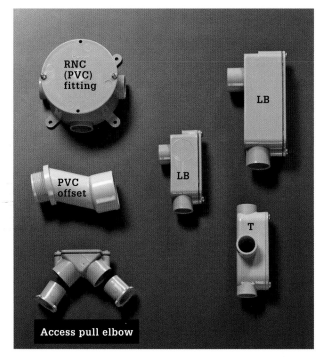

RNC (PVC) fitting

PVC offset

LB

LB

T

Access pull elbow

Nonmetallic conduit fittings typically are solvent welded to nonmetallic conduit, as opposed to metal conduit, which can be threaded and screwed into threaded fittings or attached with setscrews or compression fittings.

A thin-wall conduit bender is used to bend sweeps into EMT or IMC conduit.

How to Make Nonmetallic Conduit Connections

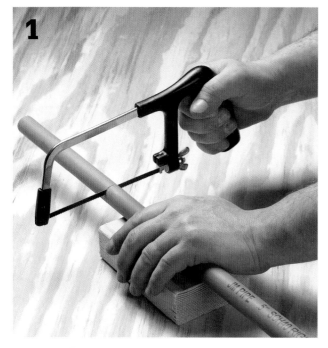

Cut the rigid nonmetallic conduit (RNC) to length with a fine-tooth saw, such as a hacksaw. For larger diameter (1½" and above), use a power miter box with a fine-tooth or plastic cutting blade.

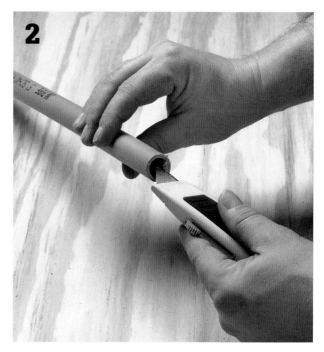

Deburr the cut edges with a utility knife or fine sandpaper such as emery paper. Wipe the cut ends with a dry rag. Also wipe the coupling or fitting to clean it.

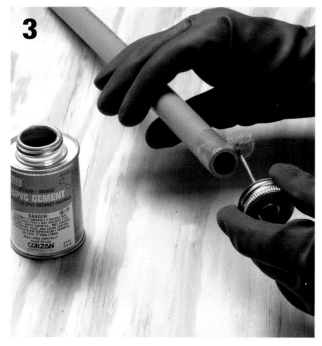

Apply a coat of PVC cement to the end of the conduit. Wear latex gloves to protect your hands. The cement should be applied past the point on the conduit where it enters the fitting or coupling.

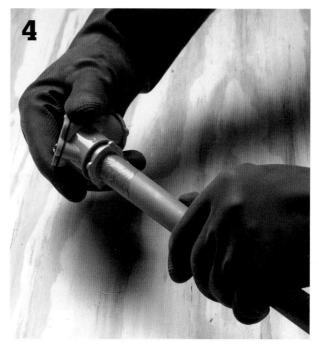

Insert the conduit into the fitting or coupling and spin it a quarter turn to help spread the cement. Allow the joint to set undisturbed for 10 minutes.

How to Install Conduit & Wires on a Concrete Wall

Measure from the floor to position electrical boxes on the wall, and mark location for mounting screws. Boxes for receptacles in an unfinished basement or other damp area are mounted at least 2 ft. from the floor. Laundry receptacles usually are mounted at 48".

Drill pilot holes with a masonry bit, then mount the box against a masonry wall with masonry anchors. Or use masonry anchors and panhead screws.

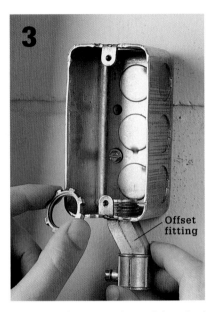

Open one knockout for each length of conduit that will be attached to the box. Attach an offset fitting to each knockout using a locknut.

Offset fitting

Measure the first length of conduit and cut it with a hacksaw. Remove any rough inside edges with a pipe reamer or a round file. Attach the conduit to the offset fitting on the box, and tighten the setscrew.

Anchor the conduit against the wall with pipe straps and masonry anchors. Conduit should be anchored within 3 ft. of each box and fitting, and every 10 ft. thereafter.

Make conduit bends by attaching a sweep fitting using a setscrew fitting or compression fitting. Continue conduit run by attaching additional lengths using setscrew or compression fittings.

Use an elbow fitting in conduit runs that have many bends, or in runs that require very long wires. The cover on the elbow fitting can be removed to make it easier to extend a fish tape and pull wires.

At the service breaker panel, turn the power off, then remove the cover and test for power. Open a knockout in the panel, then attach a setscrew fitting, and install the last length of conduit.

Unwind the fish tape and extend it through the conduit from the circuit breaker panel outward. Remove the cover on an elbow fitting when extending the fish tape around tight corners.

Trim back 2" of outer insulation from the end of the wires, then insert the wires through the loop at the tip of the fish tape.

Retrieve the wires through the conduit by pulling on the fish tape with steady pressure. *Note: Use extreme care when using a metal fish tape inside a circuit breaker panel, even when the power is turned off.*

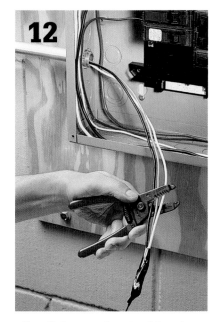

Clip off the taped ends of the wires. Leave at least 2 ft. of wire at the service panel and 8" at each electrical box.

Installing Raceway Wiring

Raceways are essentially decorative conduit. Often called surface-mounted wiring, a raceway is a track of flattened metal or plastic tubing that attaches to a wall and houses cable for a circuit. The systems include matching elbows, T-connectors, and various other fittings and boxes that are also surface-mounted. The main advantage to a raceway system is that you can add a new fixture onto a circuit without cutting into your walls.

Although they are extremely convenient and can even contribute to a room's decor when used thoughtfully, raceway systems do have some limitations. They are not allowed for some specific applications (such as damp areas like bathrooms) in many areas, so check with the local building authorities before beginning a project. And, the boxes that house the switches and receptacles tend to be very shallow and more difficult to work with than ordinary boxes.

In some cases, you may choose to run an entirely new circuit with raceway components (at least starting at the point where the feeder wire reaches the room from the service panel). But more often, a raceway circuit ties into an existing receptacle or switch. If you are tying into a standard switch box for power, make sure the load wire for the new raceway circuit is connected to the hot wire in the switch box before it is connected to the switch (otherwise, the raceway circuit will be off whenever the switch is off).

Raceway wiring systems are surface-mounted networks of electrical boxes and hollow metal tracks that allow you to expand an existing wiring circuit without cutting into your walls.

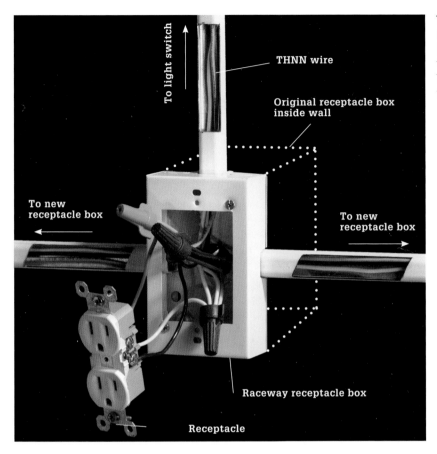

To light switch

THNN wire

Original receptacle box inside wall

To new receptacle box

To new receptacle box

Raceway receptacle box

Receptacle

The raceway receptacle box is mounted directly to the original electrical box (usually for a receptacle) and raceway tracks are attached to it. The tracks house THNN wires that run from the raceway box to new receptacles and light switches.

Parts of a Raceway System

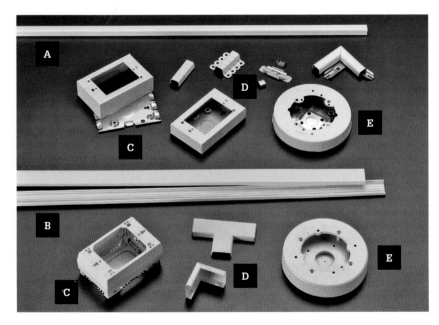

A

C

D

E

B

C

D

E

Raceway systems employ two-part tracks that are mounted directly to the wall surface to house cable. Lighter-duty plastic raceways (A), used frequently in office buildings, are made of snap-together plastic components. For home wiring, look for a heavier metal-component system (B). Both systems include box extenders for tying in to a receptacle (C), elbows, T-connectors, and couplings (D), and boxes for fixtures (E).

How to Install Raceway Wiring

Confirm that the circuit you want to expand will support a new receptacle or light. Mark the planned location of the new receptacle or switch on the wall and measure to the nearest existing receptacle. Purchase enough raceway to cover this distance plus about 10 percent extra. Buy a surface-mounted starter box, new receptacle box, and fittings for your project (the raceway product packaging usually provides guidance for shopping).

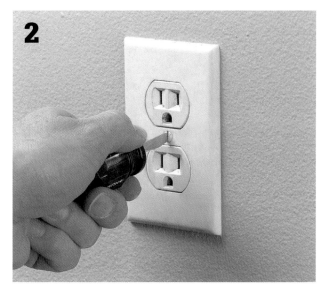

Shut off the power to the switch. Remove the cover plate from the receptacle by unscrewing the screw that holds the plate to the electrical box. Set the screws and the plate aside. With the cover plate off, you will be able to see the receptacle and the electrical box it is attached to.

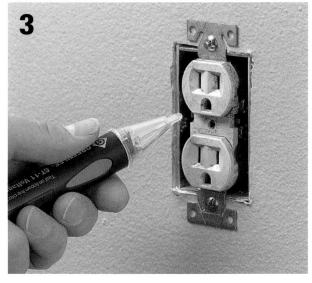

Before you remove the old receptacle, use a voltage sensor to double-check that the circuit is dead. Hold your voltage sensor's probe within ½" of the wires on each side of the receptacle. If the sensor beeps or lights up, then the receptacle is still live, and you'll need to trip the correct breaker to disconnect power to the receptacle. If the sensor does not beep or light up, the receptacle is dead and you can proceed safely.

Remove the receptacle from the box by unscrewing the two long screws that hold it to the box. Once the screws are out, gently pull the receptacle away from the box. Depending on how your receptacle has been wired, you may find two insulated wires and a bare copper wire or four insulated wires and a bare wire. Detach these wires and set the receptacle aside.

Your starter box includes a box and a mounting plate with a hole in its center. Pull all the wires you just disconnected through the hole, taking care not to scrape them on the edges of the hole. Screw the mounting plate to the existing receptacle box with the included mounting screws.

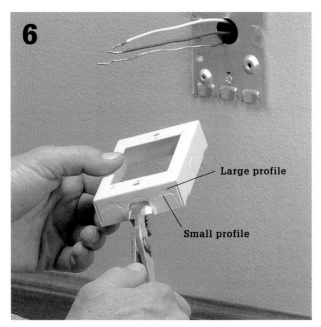

Large profile

Small profile

Remove a knockout from the starter box to create an opening for the raceway track using pliers. Often, the prepunched knockouts have two profile options—make sure the knockout you remove matches the profile of your track.

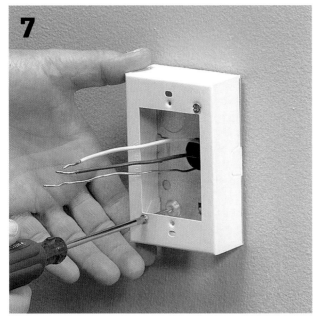

Hold the box portion of the starter box over the mounting plate on the existing receptacle. Drive the mounting screws through the holes in the box and into the threaded openings in the mounting plate.

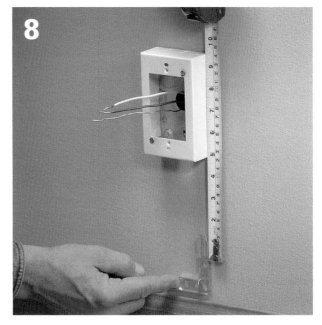

Set the mounting bracket for an elbow connector ¼" above the baseboard (having the track run along the baseboard edge looks better than running it in a straight line out of the starter box). Measure from the knockout in the starter box to the top of the bracket and cut a piece of raceway ½" longer than this measurement.

(continued)

Tool Tip ▸

Metal raceway can be cut like metal conduit. Secure the track or conduit in a vise or clamping work support and cut with a hacksaw. For best results, use long, slow strokes and don't bear down too hard on the saw.

9

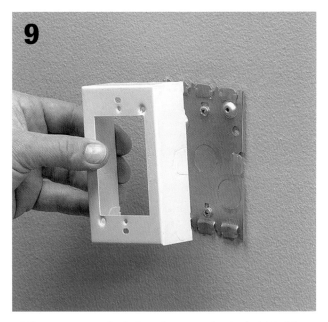

At the new receptacle location, transfer the height of the top of the starter box and mark a reference line. If possible, locate the box so at least one screw hole in the mounting plate falls over a wall stud. Position the mounting plate for the receptacle box up against the reference line and secure it with screws driven through the mounting plate holes. If the plate is not located over a wall stud, use wall anchors (see below right).

10

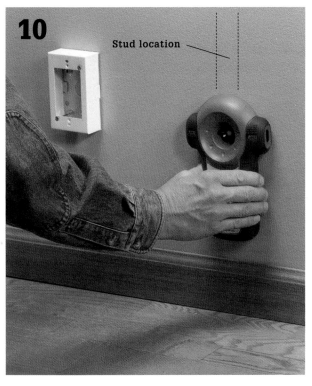

Stud location

Use a stud finder to locate and mark all of the wall framing members between the old receptacle and the new one. There is usually a 1½"-wide stud every 16" behind the wall.

Here's How ▸

Here's how to install wall anchors. Mark screw locations on the wall, then drill ¼" holes through the wall at the marks. Tap a plastic wall anchor into the hole with a hammer so the underside of the top flange is flush against the surface of the wall. When a screw is driven into the wall anchor sleeve, the sleeve will expand in the hole and hold the screw securely.

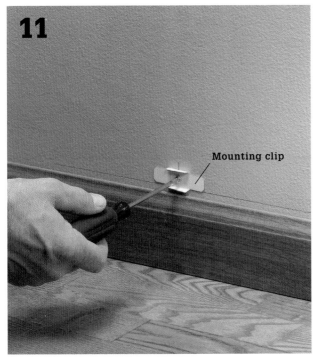

11

Mounting clip

At stud locations mark a reference line ¼" above the top of the baseboard. Attach mounting clips for the raceway track at these marks.

12

Install mounting clips ½" or so below the knockouts on both the starter box and the new receptacle box. The clips should line up with the knockouts.

13

At the starter box slide one end of the short piece of raceway into the knockout so that about ⅛" extends into the box. Snap the raceway into the clip below the knockout. Repeat this same procedure at the new receptacle box. Slip a bushing (included with installation kit) over the ends of the tracks where they enter the box.

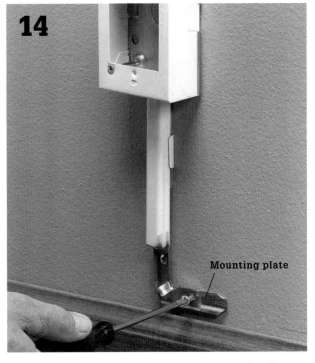

14

Mounting plate

The elbow piece will have two parts, a mounting plate and a cap. Install the mounting plates directly below the pieces of track entering the receptacle boxes.

(continued)

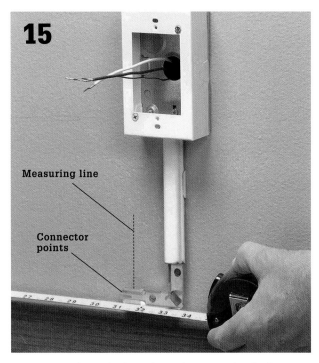

15

Measuring line

Connector points

Measure and cut the long piece of raceway that fits between the two receptacles. Measure the distance between the ends of the horizontal parts of the elbows, and cut a length of raceway to that length. Be sure to measure all the way to the base of the clip, not just to the tips of the connector points.

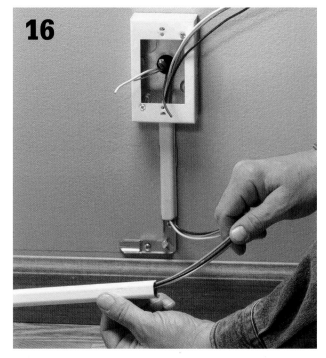

16

Cut black, white, and green THNN wire about 2-ft. longer than the length of each wiring run. Snake the end of each wire into the starter box, through the knockout, and into the vertical raceway. Then snake the wire all the way through the long piece of raceway so about 12 to 16" comes out on each end.

What If...? ▶

What if I need to go around a corner? Use corner pieces to guide raceway around corners. Corners are available for inside or outside corners and consist of a mounting plate and a cap piece. Inside corners may be used at wall/ceiling junctures.

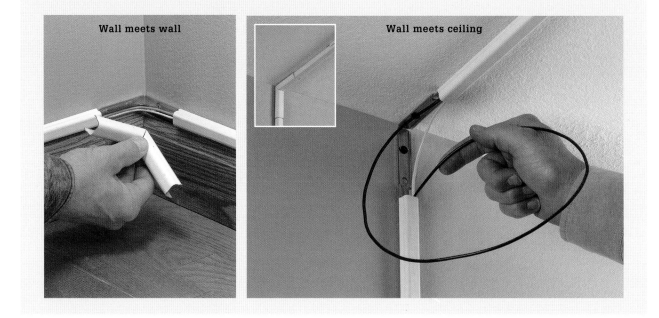

Wall meets wall

Wall meets ceiling

What If...? ▸

What if I need a piece of raceway track that's longer than the longest piece available at the hardware store (usually 5 ft.)? You can use straight connector pieces to join two lengths of raceway. Much like an elbow piece, they have a mounting plate and a cover that snaps over the wiring.

17

Snap the long piece of raceway into the mounting clips. Line up one end of the raceway with the end of an elbow and begin pressing the raceway into the clips until it is snapped into all of the clips. At the new receptacle location, snake the ends of the wires up through the vertical piece of raceway and into the new receptacle box. There should be about 6" of wire coming out at each box.

18

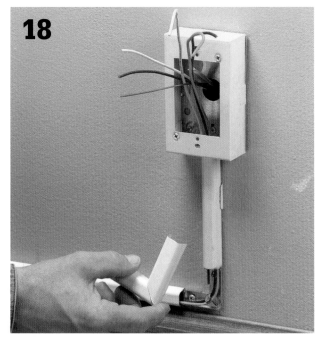

Finish the raceway by snapping the elbow cover pieces into place over the mounting plates, one at the starter box and another at the new receptacle location. You may need to rap the plate with a rubber mallet to get enough force to snap it on. Make sure all of the wire fits completely within the cover pieces.

19

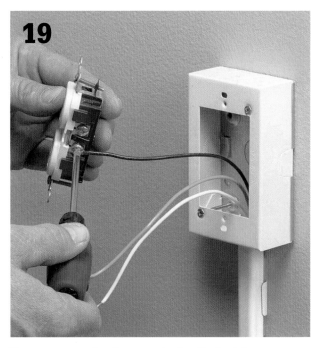

Now you can wire the receptacles. Begin at the new receptacle location. Wrap the end of the black wire around the bottom gold screw on the side of the receptacle. Tighten the screw so it's snug.

(continued)

20

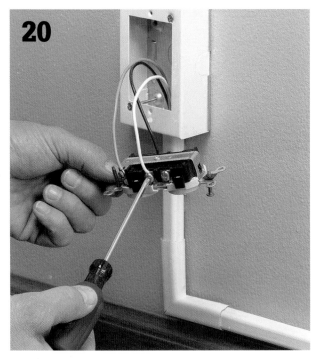

Wrap the end of the white wire around the silver screw opposite the gold one you just used. Tighten the screw so it's snug. Connect the green wire to the green-colored screw on the bottom of the receptacle.

21

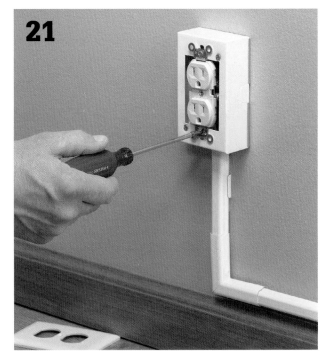

Once the connections are made, gently tuck the wires and the receptacle into the box so the holes in the top and bottom of the receptacle align with the holes in the box. Use a screwdriver to drive the two long mounting screws that hold the receptacle to the box. Attach the cover plate.

22

Now you can reinstall the old receptacle (or a replacement) at the starter box. First, make sure the power is still off with your voltage tester. Wrap the end of the black wire around the top gold screw on the side of the receptacle. Tighten the screw.

23

Wrap the end of the white wire around the silver screw opposite the gold one you just used. Tighten the screw.

24 Original receptacle

Black wire lead to new receptacle

Connect the old receptacle to the new one. Take the black wire that goes into the raceway and wrap the end of the wire around the bottom gold screw on the side of the receptacle. Tighten the screw.

25 Black wire lead to new receptacle

White wire lead to new receptacle

Wrap the end of the old white wire around the silver screw opposite the copper one you just used. Tighten the screw.

26

Finally, cut a piece of green wire about 6" long and strip ¾" from both ends (this is called a pigtail wire). Join one end of the pigtail with the ends of the bare and green wires in the box using a wire connector. Wrap the other end of the pigtail around the green screw on the receptacle.

27

Once the connections are made, tuck the wires and the receptacle into the box so the holes in the top and bottom of the receptacle align with the holes in the box. Use a screwdriver to drive the two long mounting screws that hold the receptacle to the box. Install the cover plate. You can now restore the power and test your new receptacle.

Installing Surface-mounted Wire Tape

For installing audio-video wire or low-voltage electrical supply wire, DIYers have a new option that maintains invisibility without requiring you to cut into any walls. A thin copper tape called Flatwire (made by Southwire Co., see Resources page 124) is the first wiring product that can be bonded directly to wall surfaces to run from a receptacle to a specially equipped low-voltage light fixture. Once the connections are made (using proprietary slide connectors) the wire is covered with mesh wallboard tape and then coated with joint compound and paint to conceal the wire. The company also manufacturers products, currently undergoing testing for potential code endorsement, that are designed to carry 120-volt power.

Tools & Materials ▸

Pencil	Wallboard finishing tools
Pliers	Low-voltage light fixture
Screwdrivers	Surface-mounted flat wire
Scissors	Adhesive spray
Tape measure	Fiberglass mesh tape
Smoothing knife	Plug-in transformer and
Level	connectors.

This thin copper tape is actually a code-approved conductor that can be coated with wallboard tape, joint compound and paint so you can hard-wire low-voltage lights, speakers and video displays without cutting into your walls.

How to Install Surface-mounted Wire Tape

Lay out the locations for the light fixture or fixtures. Shut off power at the main service panel and then remove the receptacle cover. Insert one end of the wire tape into the connector that attaches to the special plug-in transformer cover. Snap the connector into the back of the wall plate (supplied with the kit). Install the mounting brackets for the light fixtures before proceeding.

After attaching the wall plate to the receptacle box, spray a 3"-wide strip of adhesive in a light coat along the layout lines. Use only the adhesive provided with your kit. Read the instructions on the spray can carefully.

Beginning at the receptacle, carefully press the wire tape into the adhesive, avoiding wrinkles and air pockets. In a typical pattern, the reversible tape runs downward a few inches from the receptacle and then is folded over to make a 90° turn. Do not cut the tape.

Pressing the tape into the adhesive with a plastic smoothing tool (a broad plastic putty or wallboard knife will work—do not use metal) as you work, bond the tape to the wall up to the first fixture mounting bracket. Form a 6"-tall loop in the tape to pass over the bracket if you will be installing a second fixture. Do not cut tape if you are installing a second fixture.

Complete the installation of the wire tape and then attach a connector at the loop in the tape so the connector probes pierce the tape. The brass tabs at the ends of the wire leads from the first fixture will plug into the connector to draw power, while the tape continues uninterrupted to the second fixture.

Test the fixture after completing the connections and installing the halogen bulbs. If lights operate correctly, shut power back off, remove the fixture and transformer, and cover the wire tape with self-adhesive mesh tape (supplied with kit) and a layer of joint compound that's feathered smooth on the edges. Paint when dry.

Reinstall the fixtures and restore power. Turn the power on at the ON/OFF switch at the transformer (inset photo) first and then turn on the lights at the fixtures. If you are hanging anything on the wall near the fixtures, do not pierce the tape with fasteners.

Wiring a Room Addition

The photo below shows the circuits you would likely want to install in a large room addition. This example shows the framing and wiring of an unfinished attic converted to an office or entertainment room with a bathroom. This room includes a subpanel and five new circuits plus telephone and cable-TV lines.

A wiring project of this sort is a potentially complicated undertaking that can be made simpler by breaking the project into convenient steps, and finishing one step before moving on to the next. Turn to pages 82 to 83 to see this project represented as a wiring diagram.

Individual Circuits

■ **#1: Bathroom circuit.** This 15-amp, 120-volt circuit supplies power to bathroom fixtures and to fixtures in the adjacent closet. All general-use receptacles in a bathroom must be protected by a GFCI and a separate 20-amp circuit.

■ **#2: Computer circuit.** A 15-amp, 120-volt dedicated circuit with an extra isolated grounding wire that protects computer equipment.

Circuit breaker subpanel receives power through a 10-gauge, three-wire feeder cable connected to a 30-amp, 240-volt circuit breaker at the main circuit breaker panel.

14/2 cable

Vent fan

Vanity light fixture

GFCI receptac

Circuit breaker subpanel

12/2 cable

12/2 cable

Time & light fixture switch

14/3 cable

Blower heater

10/3 cable

Larger room additions may require a 60-amp or a 100-amp feeder circuit breaker.

#3: Air-conditioner circuit. A 20-amp, 240-volt dedicated circuit. In cooler climates, or in a smaller room, you may need an air conditioner and circuit rated for only 120 volts.

■ **#4: Basic lighting/receptacle circuit.** This 15-amp, 120-volt circuit supplies power to most of the fixtures in the bedroom and study areas.

■ **#5: Heater circuit.** This 20-amp, 240-volt circuit supplies power to the bathroom blower-heater and to the baseboard heaters. Depending on the size of your room and the wattage

rating of the baseboard heaters, you may need a 30-amp, 240-volt heating circuit.

■ **Circuit #6:** A 20-amp, 120-volt, GFCI-protected small appliance circuit for the bathroom. Includes GFCI breaker, 14/2 NM cable, boxes and 20-amp receptacles.

Telephone outlet is wired with 22-gauge four-wire phone cable. If your home phone system has two or more separate lines, you may need to run a cable with eight wires, commonly called four-pair cable.

Cable television jack is wired with coaxial cable running from an existing television junction in the utility area.

14/3 cable

14/3 cable

Phone cable

Coaxial cable

These cables continue through the foreground wall to complete the circuits. This wall has been removed for clarity.

12/2 cable

14/2 cable

Diagram View

The diagram below shows the layout of the five circuits and the locations of their receptacles, switches, fixtures, and devices as shown in the photo on the previous pages. The circuits and receptacles are based on the needs of a 400-sq.-ft. space. An inspector will want to see a diagram like this one before issuing a permit. After you've received approval for your addition, the wiring diagram will serve as your guide as you complete your project.

Circuit #1: A 15-amp, 120-volt circuit serving the bathroom and closet area. Includes: 14/2 NM cable, double-gang box, timer switch, single-pole switch, 4 × 4" box with single-gang adapter plate, two plastic light fixture boxes, vanity light fixture, closet light fixture, 15-amp single-pole circuit breaker.

Circuit #2: A 15-amp, 120-volt computer circuit. Includes: 14/3 NM cable, single-gang box, 15-amp isolated-ground receptacle, 15-amp single-pole circuit breaker.

Circuit #3: A 20-amp, 240-volt air-conditioner circuit. Includes: 12/2 NM cable; single-gang box; 20-amp,

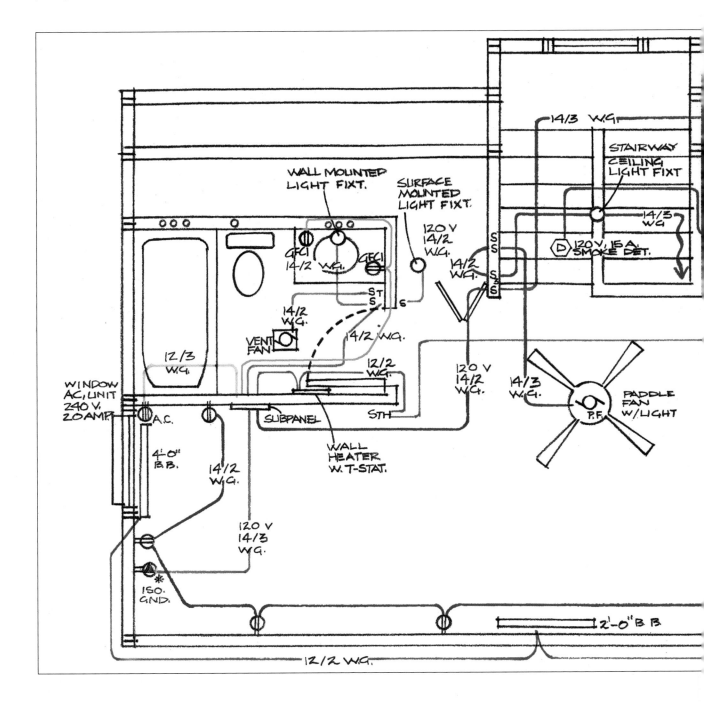

240-volt receptacle (duplex or singleplex style); 20-amp double-pole circuit.

Circuit #4: A 15-amp, 120-volt basic lighting/receptacle circuit serving most of the fixtures in the bedroom and study areas. Includes: 14/2 and 14/3 NM cable, two double-gang boxes, fan speed-control switch, dimmer switch, single-pole switch, two three-way switches, two plastic light fixture boxes, light fixture for stairway, smoke detector, metal light fixture box with brace bar, ceiling fan with light fixture, 10 single-gang boxes, 4 × 4" box with single-gang adapter plate, 10 duplex receptacles (15-amp), 15-amp single-pole circuit breaker.

Circuit #5: A 20-amp, 240-volt circuit that supplies power to three baseboard heaters controlled by a wall thermostat, and to a bathroom blower-heater controlled by a built-in thermostat. Includes: 12/2 NM cable, 750-watt blower heater, single-gang box, line-voltage thermostat, three baseboard heaters, 20-amp double-pole circuit breaker.

TV **Cable television jack:** Coaxial cable with F-connectors, signal splitter, cable television outlet with mounting brackets.

Circuit #6: A 20-amp, 120-volt, GFCI-protected small appliance circuit for the bathroom. Includes GFCI breaker, 14/2 NM cable, boxes and 20-amp receptacles.

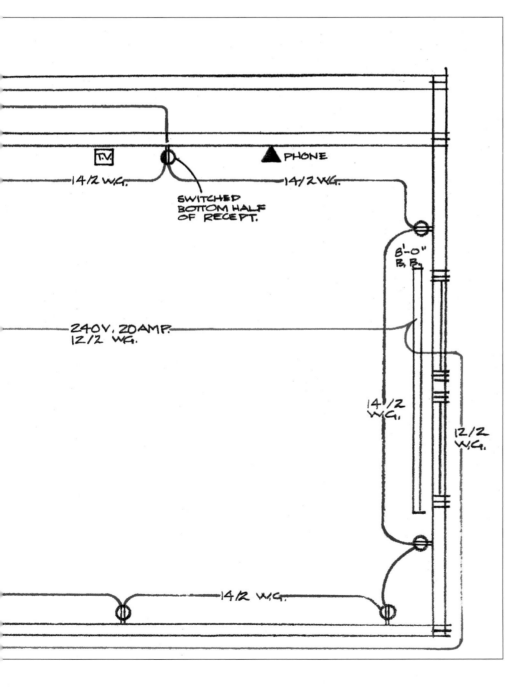

Circuit Map Details

Make the final connections for receptacles, switches, and fixtures only after the rough-in inspection is done, and all walls and ceilings are finished. The circuit maps are especially useful if your wiring configurations differ from those shown on the following pages. The last step is to hook up the new circuits at the breaker panel.

After all connections are done, your work is ready for the final inspection. If you have worked carefully, the final inspection will take only a few minutes. The inspector may open one or two electrical boxes to check wire connections, and will check the circuit breaker hookups to make sure they are correct.

Tools & Materials ▸

Combination tool
Screwdrivers
Needlenose pliers
Nut driver

Pigtail wires
Wire connectors
Green & black tape

CIRCUIT #1
A 15-amp, 120-volt circuit serving the bathroom & closet.

- Timer & single-pole switch
- Vent fan
- Two light fixtures
- GFCI receptacle
- Single-pole switch
- 15-amp single-pole circuit breaker (see pages 38 to 39 for instructions on hooking up the circuit at the circuit breaker panel)

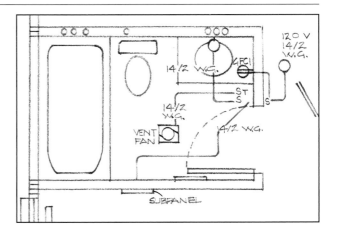

How to Connect the Timer & Single-pole Switch

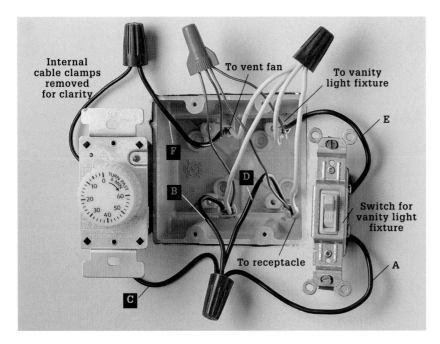

Attach a black pigtail wire (A) to one of the screw terminals on the switch. Use a wire connector to connect this pigtail to the black feed wire (B), to one of the black wire leads on the timer (C), and to the black wire carrying power to the bathroom receptacle (D). Connect the black wire leading to the vanity light fixture (E) to the remaining screw terminal on the switch. Connect the black wire running to the vent fan (F) to the remaining wire lead on the timer. Use wire connectors to join the white wires and the grounding wires. Tuck all wires into the box, then attach the switches, coverplate, and timer dial. (See also circuit map 4, page 20; and circuit map 19, page 27.)

How to Connect a Vent Fan

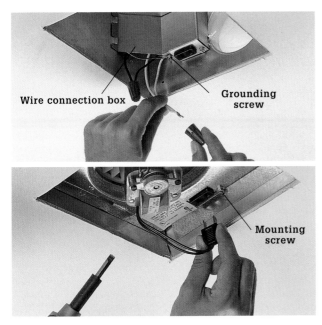

Wire connection box

Grounding screw

Mounting screw

In the wire connection box (top) connect black circuit wire to black wire lead on fan, using a wire connector. Connect white circuit wire to white wire lead. Connect grounding wire to the green grounding screw.

Insert the fan motor unit (bottom), and attach mounting screws. Connect the fan motor plug to the built-in receptacle on the wire connection box. Attach the fan grill to the frame, using the mounting clips included with the fan kit.

How to Connect Light Fixtures

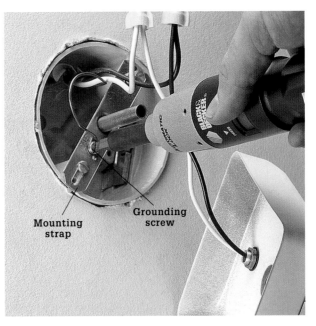

Mounting strap

Grounding screw

Attach a mounting strap with threaded nipple to the box, if required by the light fixture manufacturer. Connect the black circuit wire to the black wire lead on the light fixture, and connect the white circuit wire to the white wire lead. Connect the circuit grounding wire to the grounding screw on the mounting strap. Carefully tuck all wires into the electrical box, then position the fixture over the nipple, and attach it with the mounting nut. (See also circuit map 4, page 20.)

How to Connect the Bathroom GFCI Receptacle

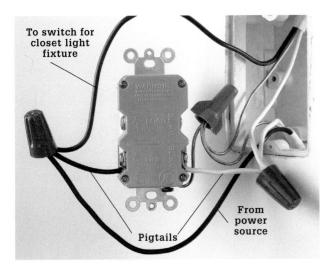

To switch for closet light fixture

From power source

Pigtails

Attach a black pigtail wire to brass screw terminal marked line. Join all black wires with a wire connector. Attach a white pigtail wire to the silver screw terminal marked line, then join all white wires with a wire connector. Attach a grounding pigtail to the green grounding screw, then join all grounding wires. Tuck all wires into the box, then attach the receptacle and the coverplate. (See also circuit map 2, page 18.)

How to Connect the Single-pole Switch

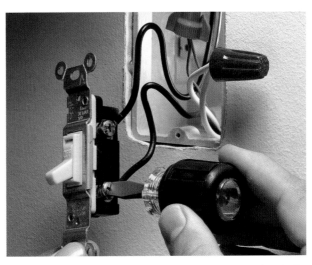

Attach the black circuit wires to the brass screw terminals on the switch. Use wire connectors to join the white neutral wires together and the bare copper grounding wires together. Tuck all wires into the box, then attach the switch and the coverplate. (See also circuit map 4, page 20.)

CIRCUIT #4
A 15-amp, 120-volt basic lighting/ receptacle circuit serving the office and bedroom areas.

- Single-pole switch for split receptacle, three-way switch for stairway light fixture
- Speed-control and dimmer switches for ceiling fan
- Switched duplex receptacle
- 15-amp, 120-volt receptacles
- Ceiling fan with light fixture
- Smoke detector
- Stairway light fixture
- 15-amp single-pole circuit breaker (see pages 38 to 39)

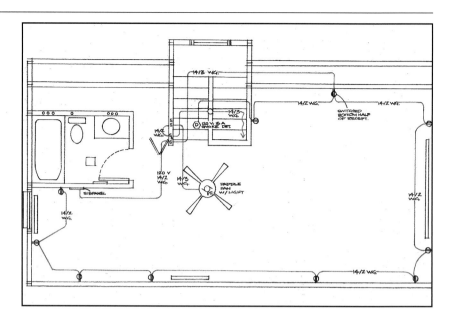

How to Connect Switches for Receptacle & Stairway Light

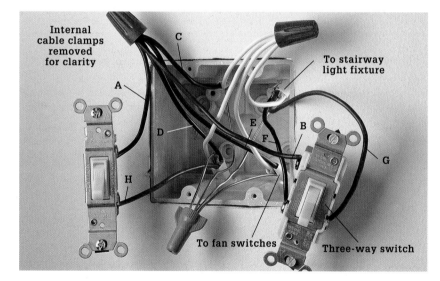

Attach a black pigtail wire (A) to one of the screws on the single-pole switch and another black pigtail (B) to common screw on three-way switch. Use a wire connector to connect pigtail wires to black feed wire (C), to black wire running to unswitched receptacles (D), and to the black wire running to fan switches (E). Connect remaining wires running to light fixture (F, G) to traveler screws on three-way switch. Connect red wire running to switched receptacle (H) to remaining screw on single-pole switch. Use wire connectors to join white wires and grounding wires. Tuck all wires into box, then attach switches and coverplate. (See also circuit map 7, page 21; and map 18, page 27.)

How to Connect the Ceiling Fan Switches

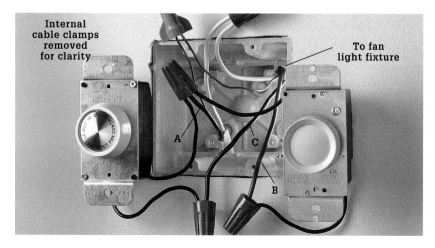

Connect the black feed wire (A) to one of the black wire leads on each switch, using a wire connector. Connect the red circuit wire (B) running to the fan light fixture to the remaining wire lead on the dimmer switch. Connect the black circuit wire (C) running to the fan motor to the remaining wire lead on the speed-control switch. Use wire connectors to join the white wires and the grounding wires. Tuck all wires into the box, then attach the switches, coverplate, and switch dials. (See also circuit map 30, page 33.)

How to Connect a Switched Receptacle

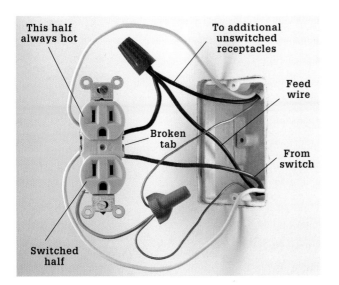

Break the connecting tab between the brass screw terminals on the receptacle, using needlenose pliers. Attach the red wire to the bottom brass screw. Connect a black pigtail wire to the other brass screw, then connect all black wires with a wire connector. Connect white wires to silver screws. Attach a grounding pigtail to the green grounding screw, then join all the grounding wires, using a wire connector. Tuck the wires into the box, then attach the receptacle and coverplate (See also circuit map 7, page 21.)

How to Connect Receptacles

Connect the black circuit wires to the brass screw terminals on the receptacle, and the white wires to the silver terminals. Attach a grounding pigtail to the green grounding screw on the receptacle, then join all grounding wires with a wire connector. Tuck the wires into the box, then attach the receptacle and coverplate. (See also circuit map 1, page 18.)

How to Connect a Ceiling Fan/Light Fixture

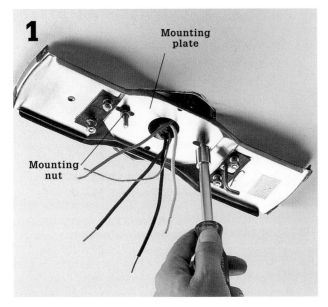

Place the ceiling fan mounting plate over the stove bolts extending through the electrical box. Pull the circuit wires through the hole in the center of the mounting plate. Attach the mounting nuts, and tighten them with a nut driver.

Hang fan motor from mounting hook. Connect black circuit wire to black wire lead from fan, using a wire connector. Connect red circuit wire from dimmer to blue wire lead from light fixture, white circuit wire to white lead, and grounding wires to green lead. Complete assembly of fan and light fixture, following manufacturer's directions. (See also circuit map 30, page 33.)

■ CIRCUIT #5
A 20-amp, 240-volt circuit serving the bathroom blower-heater and three baseboard heaters controlled by a wall thermostat.

- 240-volt blower-heater
- 240-volt thermostat
- 240-volt baseboard heaters
- 20-amp double-pole circuit breaker (see pages 38 to 39 for instructions on hooking up the circuit at the circuit breaker panel)

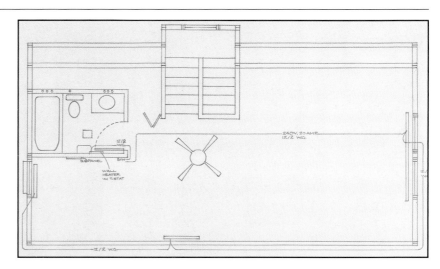

■ How to Connect a 240-volt Blower-Heater

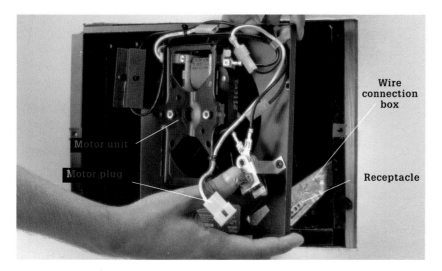

Blower-heaters: In the heater's wire connection box, connect one of the wire leads to the white circuit wires, and the other wire lead to the black circuit wires, using same method as for baseboard heaters (page, opposite). Insert the motor unit, and attach the motor plug to the built-in receptacle. Attach the coverplate and thermostat knob. Note: Some types of blower-heaters can be wired for either 120 volts or 240 volts. If you have this type, make sure the internal plug connections are configured for 240 volts.

■ How to Connect a 240-volt Thermostat

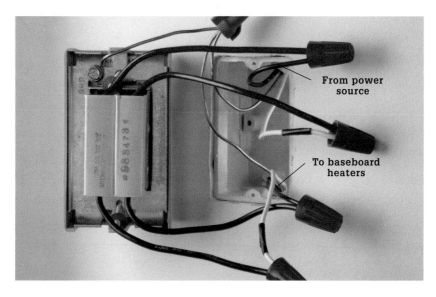

Connect the red wire leads on the thermostat to the circuit wires entering the box from the power source, using wire connectors. Connect black wire leads to circuit wires leading to the baseboard heaters. Tag the white wires with black tape to indicate they are hot. Attach a grounding pigtail to the grounding screw on the thermostat, then connect all grounding wires. Tuck the wires into the box, then attach the thermostat and coverplate. (See also circuit map 15, page 25.) Follow manufacturer's directions: the color coding for thermostats may vary.

How to Connect 240-volt Baseboard Heaters

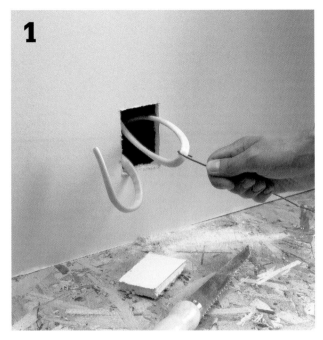

At the cable location, cut a small hole in the wallboard, 3" to 4" above the floor, using a wallboard saw. Pull the cables through the hole, using a piece of stiff wire with a hook on the end. Middle-of-run heaters will have 2 cables, while end-of-run heaters have only 1 cable.

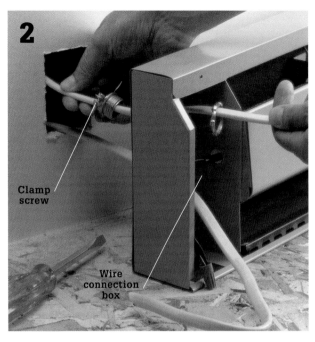

Clamp screw

Wire connection box

Remove the cover on the wire connection box. Open a knockout for each cable that will enter the box, then feed the cables through the cable clamps and into the wire connection box. Attach the clamps to the wire connection box, and tighten the clamp screws until the cables are gripped firmly.

Anchor heater against wall, about 1" off floor, by driving flat-head screws through back of housing and into studs. Strip away cable sheathing so at least ¼" of sheathing extends into the heater. Strip ¾" of insulation from each wire, using a combination tool.

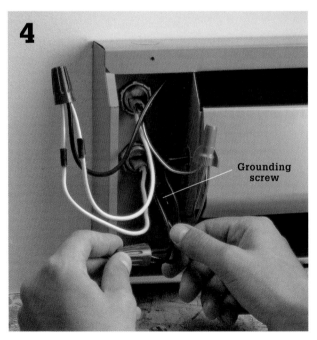

Grounding screw

Use wire connectors to connect the white circuit wires to one of the wire leads on the heater. Tag white wires with black tape to indicate they are hot. Connect the black circuit wires to the other wire lead. Connect a grounding pigtail to the green grounding screw in the box, then join all grounding wires with a wire connector. Reattach cover. (See also circuit map 15, page 25.)

Wiring a Kitchen Remodel

14/2 cable

14/2 cable

12/3 cable

12/2 cable

6/3 cable

14/3 cable

14/2 cable

14/2 cable

12/3 cable

12/3 cable

14/2 cable

The photo at left shows the circuits you would probably want to install in a total kitchen remodel. Kitchens require a wide range of electrical services, from simple 15-amp lighting circuits to 120/240, 60-amp appliance circuits. This kitchen example has seven circuits, including separate dedicated circuits for a dishwasher and food disposer. Some codes allow the disposer and dishwasher to share a single circuit.

All rough carpentry and plumbing should be in place before beginning any electrical work. As always, divide a project of this scale into manageable steps, and finish one step before moving on. Turn to pages 92 to 93 to see this project represented as a wiring diagram.

Individual Circuits

■ **#1 & #2: Small-appliance circuits.** Two 20-amp, 120-volt circuits supply power to countertop and eating areas for small appliances. All general-use receptacles must be on these circuits. One 12/3 cable fed by a 20-amp double-pole breaker wires both circuits. These circuits share one electrical box with the disposer circuit (#5), and another with the basic lighting circuit (#7).

■ **#3: Range circuit.** A 50-amp, 120/240-volt dedicated circuit supplies power to the range/ oven appliance. It is wired with 6/3 cable.

■ **#4: Microwave circuit.** A dedicated 20-amp, 120-volt circuit supplies power to the microwave. It is wired with 12/2 cable. Microwaves that use less than 300 watts can be installed on a 15-amp circuit or plugged into the small-appliance circuits.

■ **#5: Food disposer/dishwasher circuit.** A dedicated 15-amp, 120-volt circuit supplies power to the disposer. It is wired with 14/2 cable. Some local codes allow disposer to be on the same circuit as the dishwasher.

■ **#6: Dishwasher circuit.** A 15-amp, 120-volt dedicated circuit for the dishwasher is wired with 14/2 cable.

■ **#7: Basic lighting circuit.** A 15-amp, 120-volt circuit powers the ceiling fixture, recessed fixtures, and undercabinet task lights. 14/2 and 14/3 cables connect the fixtures and switches in the circuit. Each task light has a self-contained switch.

Diagram View

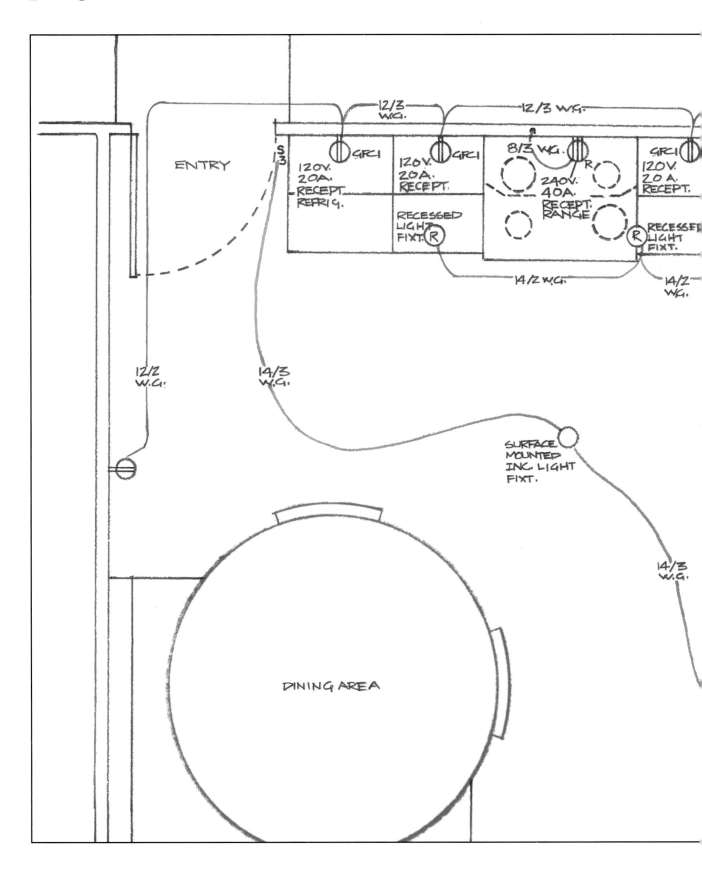

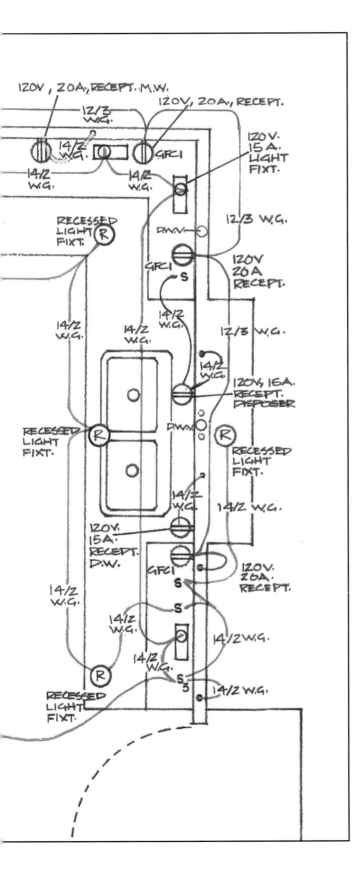

The diagram at left shows the layout of the seven circuits and the locations of their receptacles, switches, fixtures, and devices as shown in the photo on the previous pages. The circuits and receptacles are based on the needs of a 175-sq.-ft. space kitchen. An inspector will want to see a diagram like this one before issuing a permit. After you've received approval for your addition, the wiring diagram will serve as your guide as you complete your project.

■ **Circuits #1 & #2:** Two 20-amp, 120-volt small-appliance circuits wired with one cable. All general-use receptacles must be on these circuits, and they must be GFCI units. Includes: seven GFCI receptacles rated for 20 amps, five electrical boxes that are 4 × 4", and 12/3 cable. One GFCI shares a double-gang box with circuit #5, and another GFCI shares a triple-gang box with circuit #7.

■ **Circuit #3:** A 50-amp, 120/240-volt dedicated circuit for the range. Includes: a 4 × 4" box; a 120/240-volt, 50-amp range receptacle; and 6/3 NM cable.

■ **Circuit #4:** A 20-amp, 120-volt dedicated circuit for the microwave. Includes: a 20-amp duplex receptacle, a single-gang box, and 12/2 NM cable.

■ **Circuit #5:** A 15-amp, 120-volt dedicated circuit for the food disposer. Includes: a 15-amp duplex receptacle, a single-pole switch (installed in a double-gang box with a GFCI receptacle from the small-appliance circuits), one single-gang box, and 14/2 cable.

■ **Circuit #6:** A 15-amp, 120-volt dedicated circuit for the dishwasher. Includes: a 15-amp duplex receptacle, one single-gang box, and 14/2 cable.

■ **Circuit #7:** A 15-amp, 120-volt basic lighting circuit serving all of the lighting needs in the kitchen. Includes: two single-pole switches, two three-way switches, single-gang box, 4 × 4" box, triple-gang box (shared with one of the GFCI receptacles from the small-appliance circuits), plastic light fixture box with brace, ceiling light fixture, four fluorescent undercabinet light fixtures, six recessed light fixtures, 14/2 and 14/3 cables.

Circult Map Details

Make the final connections for switches, receptacles, and fixtures after the rough-in inspection. First make final connections on recessed fixtures (it is easier to do this before wallboard is installed). Then finish the work on walls and ceiling, install the cabinets, and make the rest of the final connections. Use the photos on the following pages and the circuit maps on pages 18 to 33 as a guide for making the final connections. The last step is to connect the circuits at the breaker panel (pages 38 to 39). After all connections are made, your work is ready for the final inspection.

Tools & Materials ▸

Pigtail wires   Black tape
Wire connectors

■ CIRCUITS #1 & #2
Two 20-amp, 120-volt small-appliance circuits.

- 7 GFCI receptacles
- 20-amp double-pole circuit breaker (see pages 38 to 39 for instructions on making final connections at the circuit breaker panel)

Note: In this project, two of the GFCI receptacles are installed in boxes that also contain switches from other circuits (page opposite).

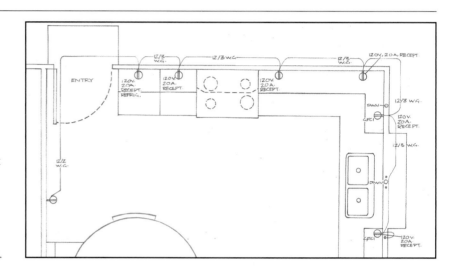

How to Connect Small-appliance Receptacles (two alternating 20-amp circuits in one 12/3 cable)

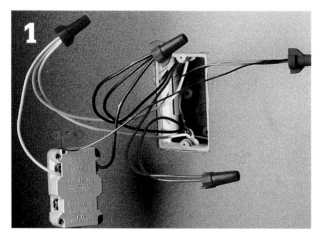

At alternate receptacles in the cable run (first, third, etc.), attach a black pigtail to a brass screw terminal marked line on the receptacle and to black wire from both cables. Connect a white pigtail to a silver screw (line) and to both white wires. Connect a grounding pigtail to the grounding screw and to both grounding wires. Connect both red wires together. Tuck wires into box, then attach the receptacle and coverplate. (See circuit map 13, page 24.)

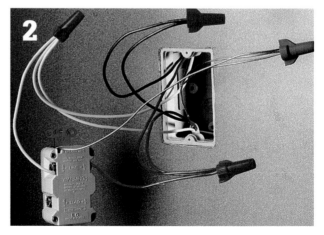

At remaining receptacles in the run, attach a red pigtail to a brass screw terminal (line) and to red wires from the cables. Attach a white pigtail to a silver screw terminal (line) and to both white wires. Connect a grounding pigtail to the grounding screw and to both grounding wires. Connect both black wires together. Tuck wires into box, attach receptacle and coverplate.

How to Install a GFCI & a Disposer Switch

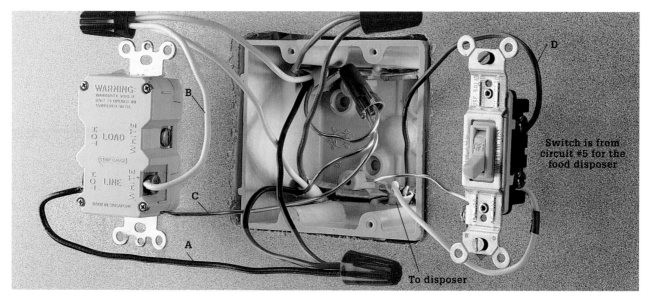

Connect black pigtail (A) to GFCI brass terminal marked line, and to black wires from three-wire cables. Attach white pigtail (B) to silver terminal marked line, and to white wires from three-wire cables. Attach grounding pigtail (C) to GFCI grounding screw and to grounding wires from three-wire cables. Connect both red wires together. (See circuit map 11, page 23.) Connect black wire from two-wire cable (D) to one switch terminal. Attach white wire to other terminal, and tag it black indicating it is hot. Attach grounding wire to switch grounding screw. (See circuit map 5, page 20.) Tuck wires into box; attach switch, receptacle, and coverplate.

How to Install a GFCI & Two Switches for Recessed Lights

Connect red pigtail (A) to GFCI brass terminal labeled line, and to red wires from three-wire cables. Connect white pigtail (B) to silver line terminal and to white wires from three-wire cables. Attach grounding pigtail (C) to grounding screw and to grounding wires from three-wire cables. Connect black wires from three-wire cables (D) together. (See circuit map 11, page 23.) Attach a black pigtail to one screw on each switch and to black wire from two-wire feed cable (E). Connect black wire (F) from the two-wire cable leading to recessed lights to remaining screw on the switch for the recessed lights. Connect black wire (G) from two-wire cable leading to sink light to remaining screw on sink light switch. Connect white wires from all two-wire cables together. Connect pigtails to switch grounding screws and to all grounding wires from two-wire cables. (See circuit map 4, page 19.) Tuck wires into box; attach switches, receptacle, and coverplate.

CIRCUIT #3
A 50-amp, 120/240-volt circuit serving the range.

- 50-amp receptacle for range
- 50-amp double-pole circuit breaker (see pages 38 to 39 for instructions on making final connections at the circuit breaker panel)

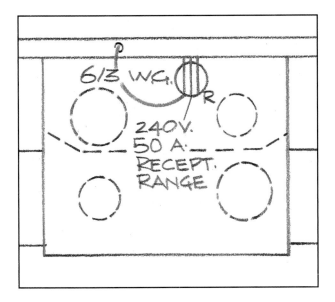

How to Install 120/240 Range Receptacle

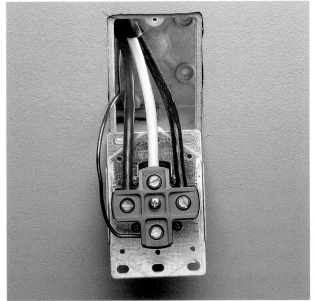

Attach the white wire to the neutral terminal, and the black and red wires to the remaining terminals. Attach the bare copper grounding wire to the grounding screw on the receptacle. Attach receptacle and coverplate. (See circuit map 14, page 25.)

CIRCUIT #4
A 20-amp, 120-volt circuit for the microwave.

- 20-amp duplex receptacle
- 20-amp single-pole circuit breaker (see pages 38 to 39 for instructions on making final connections at the circuit breaker panel)

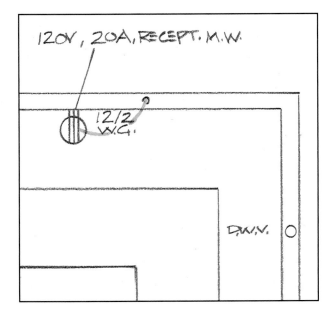

How to Connect Microwave

Connect black wire from the cable to a brass screw terminal on the receptacle. Attach the white wire to a silver screw terminal and the grounding wire to the receptacle's grounding screw. Tuck wires into box, then attach the receptacle and the coverplate. (See circuit map 1, page 18.)

■ CIRCUIT #5
A 15-amp, 120-volt circuit for the food disposer.

- 15-amp duplex receptacle
- Single-pole switch
- 15-amp single-pole circuit breaker

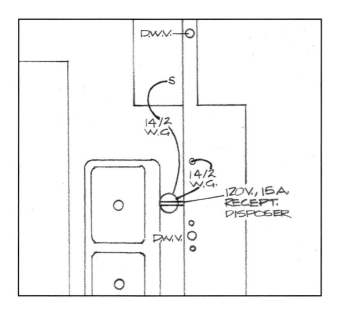

■ How to Connect Disposer Receptacle

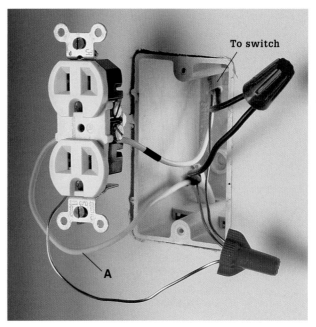

Connect black wires together. Connect white wire from feed cable (A) to silver screw on receptacle. Connect white wire from cable going to the switch to a brass screw terminal on the receptacle, and tag the wire with black indicating it is hot. Attach a grounding pigtail to grounding screw and to both cable grounding wires. Tuck wires into box, then attach receptacle and coverplate. (See circuit map 5, page 20.)

■ CIRCUIT #6
A 15-amp, 120-volt circuit for the dishwasher.

- 15-amp duplex receptacle
- 15-amp single-pole circuit breaker (see pages 38 to 39 for instructions on making final connections at the circuit breaker panel)

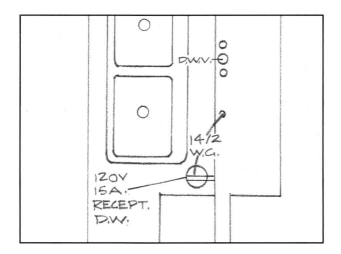

■ How to Connect Dishwasher Receptacle

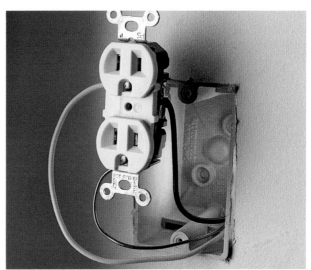

Connect the black wire to a brass screw terminal. Attach the white wire to a silver screw terminal. Connect the grounding wire to the grounding screw. Tuck wires into box, then attach receptacle and coverplate. (See circuit map 1, page 18.)

A 15-amp basic lighting circuit serving the kitchen.

- 2 three-way switches with grounding screws
- 2 single-pole switches with grounding screws
- Ceiling light fixture
- 6 recessed light fixtures
- 4 fluorescent under-cabinet fixtures
- 15-amp single-pole circuit breaker (pages 38 to 39)

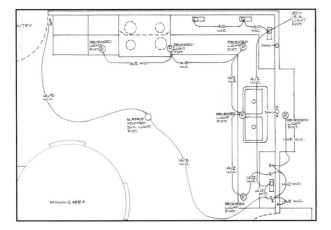

How to Connect First Three-way Switch

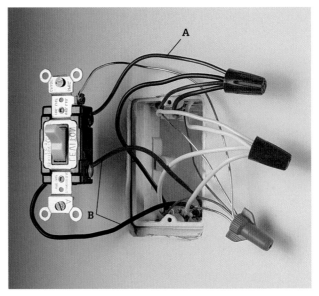

Connect a black pigtail to the common screw on the switch (A) and to the black wires from the two-wire cable. Connect black and red wires from the three-wire cable to traveler terminals (B) on the switch. Connect white wires from all cables entering box together. Attach a grounding pigtail to switch grounding screw and to all grounding wires in box. Tuck wires into box, then attach switch and coverplate. (See circuit map 20, page 28.)

How to Connect Surface-mounted Ceiling Fixture

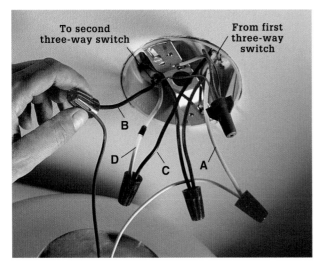

Connect white fixture lead to white wire (A) from first three-way switch. Connect black fixture lead to black wire (B) from second three-way switch. Connect black wire (C) from first switch to white wire (D) from second switch, and tag this white wire with black. Connect red wires from both switches together. Connect all grounding wires together. Mount fixture following manufacturer's instructions. (See circuit map 20, page 28.)

How to Connect Second Three-way Switch

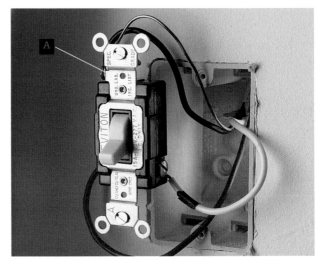

Connect black wire from the cable to the common screw terminal (A). Connect red wire to one traveler screw terminal. Attach the white wire to the other traveler screw terminal, and tag it with black indicating it is hot. Attach the grounding wire to the grounding screw on the switch. Tuck wires in box, then attach switch and coverplate. (See circuit map 20, page 28.)

How to Install Under-cabinet Lights

1

Drill ⅝" holes through wall and cabinet at locations that line up with knockouts on the fixture, and retrieve cable ends.

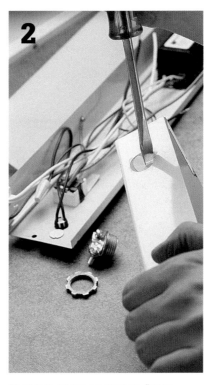

2

Remove access cover on fixture. Open one knockout for each cable that enters fixture box, and install cable clamps.

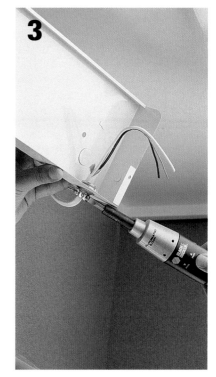

3

Strip 8" of sheathing from each cable end. Insert each end through a cable clamp, leaving ¼" of sheathing in fixture box.

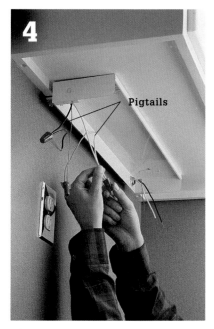

4

Screw fixture box to cabinet. Attach black, white, and green pigtails of THHN/ THWN wire to wires from one cable entering box. Pigtails must be long enough to reach the cable at other end of box.

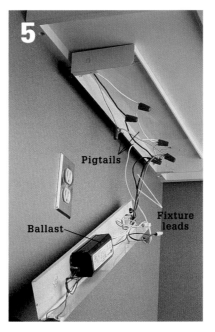

5

Connect black pigtail and circuit wire to black lead from fixture. Connect white pigtail and circuit wire to white lead from fixture. Attach green pigtail and copper circuit wire to green grounding wire attached to the fixture box.

6

Tuck wires into box, and route THHN/THWN pigtails along one side of the ballast. Replace access cover and fixture lens.

Wiring an Outbuilding

Nothing improves the convenience and usefulness of an outbuilding more than electrifying it. Running a new underground circuit from your house to an outbuilding lets you add receptacles and light fixtures both inside the outbuilding and on its exterior.

Adding an outdoor circuit is not complicated, but every aspect of the project is strictly governed by local building codes. Therefore, once you've mapped out the job and have a good idea of what's involved, visit your local building department to discuss your plans and obtain a permit for the work.

This project demonstrates standard techniques for running a circuit cable from the house exterior to a shed, plus the wiring and installation of devices inside the shed. To add a new breaker and make the final circuit connections to your home's main service panel, see page 38. The building department may recommend or require using a GFCI breaker to protect the entire circuit. Alternatively, you may be allowed to provide GFCI protection to the circuit devices via the receptacle inside the shed. GFCI protection is required on all outdoor circuits.

For basic electrical needs, such as powering a standard light fixture and small appliances or power tools, a 15-amp circuit should be sufficient. However, if you plan to run power-hungry equipment like stationary woodworking or welding tools, you may need one or more dedicated 20-amp circuits. Also, if the shed is more than 50 ft. away from the house, you may need heavier-gauge cable to account for voltage drop.

Most importantly, don't forget to call before you dig. Have all utility and service lines on your property marked even before you make serious project plans. This is critical for your safety, of course, and it may affect where you can run the circuit cable.

Adding an electrical circuit to an outbuilding like this shed greatly expands the activities the building will support and is also a great benefit for home security.

Tools & Materials ▸

Spray paint
Trenching shovel
   (4" wide blade)
4" Metal junction box
Metal L-fittings (2)
   and conduit nipple
   for IMC conduit
Wood screws
IMC conduit
   with watertight
   threaded and
   compression fittings
Wrenches

Hacksaw
90° sweeps for IMC
   conduit (2)
Plastic conduit
   bushings (2)
Pipe straps
Silicone caulk
   and caulk gun
Double-gang
   boxes, metal (2)
One exterior
   receptacle box
   (with cover)

Single-pole switches (2)
Interior ceiling light
   fixture and metal
   fixture box
Exterior motion
   detector fixture and
   plastic fixture box
EMT metal conduit
   and fittings for
   inside the shed
Utility knife
UF two-wire cable
   (12 gauge)

NM two-wire cable
   (12 gauge)
15 amp GFI protected
   circuit breaker
Wire stripper
Pliers
Screwdrivers
Wire connectors
Hand tamper

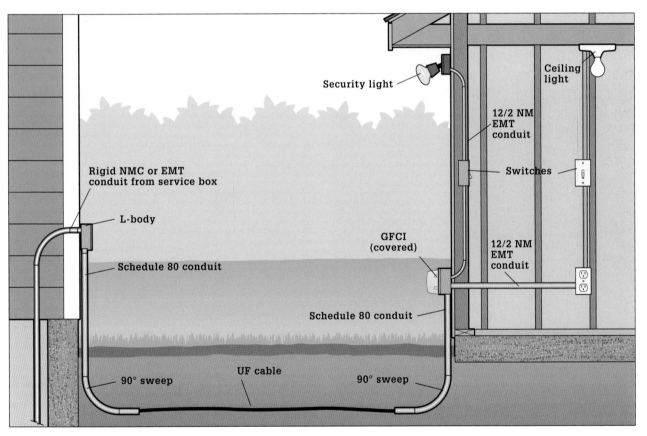

A basic outdoor circuit starts with a waterproof fitting at the house wall connected to a junction box inside. The underground circuit cable—rated UF (underground feeder)—runs in an 18"- to 24"-deep trench and is protected from exposure at both ends by metal or PVC conduit. Inside the shed, standard NM cable runs through metal conduit to protect it from damage (not necessary if you will be adding interior wallcoverings). All receptacles and devices in the shed must be GFCI protected.

How to Wire an Outbuilding

Identify the circuit's exit point at the house and entry point at the shed and mark them. Mark the path of the trench between the exit and entry points using spray paint. Make the route as direct as possible. Dig the trench to the depth required by local code using a narrow trenching shovel.

From outside, drill a hole through the exterior wall and the rim joist at the exit point for the cable (you'll probably need to install a bit extender or an extralong bit in your drill). Make the hole just large enough to accommodate the L-body conduit fitting and conduit nipple.

Assemble the conduit and junction box fittings that will penetrate the wall. Here, we attached a 12" piece of ¾" IMC (intermediate metallic conduit) and a sweep to a metal junction box with a compression fitting, and then inserted the conduit into the hole drilled in the rim joist. The junction box is attached to the floor joist.

From outside, seal the hole around the conduit with expandable spray foam or caulk, and then attach the free end of the conduit to the back of a waterproof L-body fitting. Mount the L-body fitting to the house exterior with the open end facing downward.

Cut a length of IMC to extend from the L-fitting down into the trench using a hacksaw. Deburr the cut edges of the conduit. Secure the conduit to the L-fitting, then attach a 90° sweep to the bottom end of the conduit using compression fittings. Add a bushing to the end of the sweep to protect the circuit cable. Anchor the conduit to the wall with a corrosion-resistant pipe strap.

Inside the shed, drill a ¾" dia. hole in the shed wall. On the interior of the shed, mount a junction box with an open back to allow the cable to enter through the hole. On the exterior side directly above the end of the UF trench, mount an exterior-rated receptacle box with cover. The plan (and your plan likely will differ) is to bring power into the shed through the hole in the wall behind the exterior receptacle.

Run IMC from the exterior box down into the trench. Fasten the conduit to the building with a strap. Add a 90° sweep and bushing, as before. Secure the conduit to the box with an offset fitting. Anchor the conduit with pipe straps, and seal the entry hole with caulk.

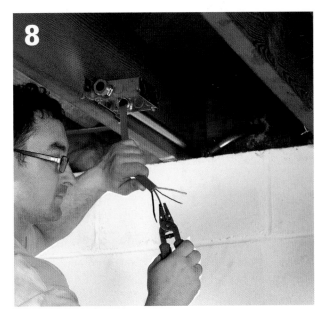

Run UF (underground feeder) cable from the house to the outbuilding. Feed one end of the UF circuit cable up through the sweep and conduit and into the L-fitting at the house (the back or side of the fitting is removable to facilitate cabling). Run the cable through the wall and into the junction box, leaving at least 12" of extra cable at the end.

(continued)

Lay the UF cable into the trench, making sure it is not twisted and will not contact any sharp objects. Roll out the cable and then feed the other end of the cable up through the conduit and into the receptacle box in the shed, leaving 12" of slack.

Inside the outbuilding, install the remaining boxes for the other switches, receptacles, and lights. With the exception of plastic receptacle boxes for exterior exposure, use metal boxes if you will be connecting the boxes with metal conduit.

Connect the electrical boxes with conduit and fittings. Inside the outbuilding, you may use inexpensive EMT to connect receptacle, switch, and fixture boxes. Once you've planned your circuit routes, start by attaching couplings to all of the boxes.

Cut a length of conduit to fit between the coupling and the next box or fitting in the run. If necessary, drill holes for the conduit through the centers of the wall studs. Attach the conduit to the fitting that you attached to the first box.

13

If you are surface-mounting the conduit or running it up or down next to wall studs, secure it with straps no more than 3 ft. apart. Use elbow fittings for 90° turns and setscrew couplings for joining straight lengths as needed. Make holes through the wall studs only as large as necessary to feed the conduit through.

14

Measure to find how much NM cable you'll need for each run, and cut a piece that's a foot or two longer. Before making L-turns with the conduit, feed the cable through the first conduit run.

15

Feed the other end of the cable into the next box or fitting in line. It is much easier to feed cable into 45° and 90° elbows if they have not been attached to the conduit yet. Continue feeding cable into the conduit and fitting until you have reached the next box in line.

16

Once you've reached the next box in line, coil the end of the cable and repeat the process with new cable for the next run. Keep working until all of the cable is run and all of the conduit and fittings are installed and secured. If you are running multiple cables into a single box, write the origin or destination on a piece of masking tape and stick it to each cable end.

(continued)

17

Make the wiring connections at the receptacles. Strip ¾" of insulation from the circuit wires using a wire stripper. Connect the white (neutral) wire and black (hot) wire of the UF cable to the LINE screw terminals on the receptacle. Connect the white (neutral) and black (hot) wires from the NM cable to the LOAD terminals. Pigtail the bare copper ground wires and connect them to the receptacle ground terminal and the metal box. Install the receptacle and cover plate.

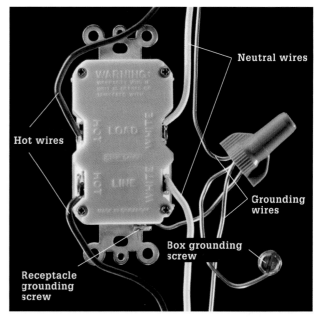

Neutral wires

Hot wires

Grounding wires

Box grounding screw

Receptacle grounding screw

Variation: Installing a GFCI-protected breaker for the new circuit at the main service panel is the best way to protect the circuit and allows you to use regular receptacles in the building, but an alternative that is allowed in many areas is to run the service into a GFCI-protected receptacle and then wire the other devices on the circuit in series. If you use this approach, only the initial receptacle needs to be GFCI protected.

18

Continue installing receptacles in the circuit run, and then run service from the last receptacle to the switch box for the light fixture or fixtures. (If you anticipate a lot of load on the circuit, you should probably run a separate circuit for the lights). Twist the white neutral leads and grounding leads together and cap them. Attach the black wires to the appropriate switches. Install the switches and cover plate.

19

Install the light fixtures. For this shed, we installed a caged ceiling light inside the shed and a motion-detector security light on the exterior side.

Run NM cable from the electrical box in the house at the start of the new circuit to the main service panel. Use cable staples if you are running the cable in floor joist cavities. If the cable is mounted to the bottom of the floor joists or will be exposed, run it through conduit.

At the service panel, feed the NM cable in through a cable clamp. Arrange for your final electrical inspection before you install the breaker. Then attach the wires to a new circuit breaker and install the breaker in an empty slot. Label the new circuit on the circuit map.

Turn on the new circuit and test all of the receptacles and fixtures. Depress the Test button and then the Reset button if you installed a GFCI receptacle. If any of the fixtures or receptacles is not getting power, check the connections first and then test the receptacle or switch for continuity with a multimeter.

Lay narrow scraps of lumber over the cable in the trench as an extra layer of protection from digging and then backfill with dirt to cover. Replace the sod in the trench if you saved it.

Motion-sensing Floodlights

Most houses and garages have floodlights on their exteriors. You can easily upgrade these fixtures so that they provide additional security by replacing them with motion-sensing floodlights. Motion-sensing floods can be set up to detect motion in a specific area—like a walkway or driveway—and then cast light into that area. And there are few things intruders like less than the spotlight. These lights typically have timers that allow you to control how long the light stays on and photosensors that prevent the light from coming on during the day.

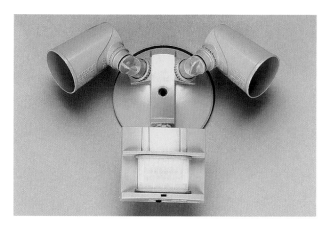

A motion-sensing light fixture provides inexpensive and effective protection against intruders. It has an infrared eye that triggers the light fixture when a moving object crosses its path. Choose a light fixture with: a photo cell to prevent the light from turning on in daylight; an adjustable timer to control how long the light stays on; and range control to adjust the reach of the motion-sensor eye.

An exterior floodlight with a motion sensor is an effective security measure. Keep the motion sensor adjusted to cover only the area you wish to secure—if the coverage area is too large the light will turn on frequently.

How to Install a New Exterior Fixture Box

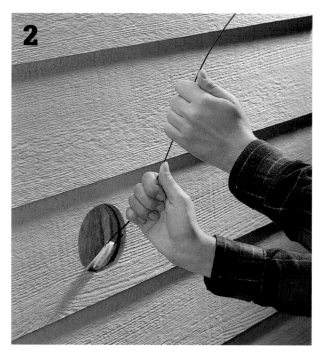

On the outside of the house, make the cutout for the motion-sensor light fixture. Outline the light fixture box on the wall, then drill a pilot hole and complete the cutout with a wallboard saw or jigsaw.

Estimate the distance between the indoor switch box and the outdoor motion-sensor box, and cut a length of NM cable about 2 ft. longer than this distance. Use a fish tape to pull the cable from the switch box to the motion-sensor box.

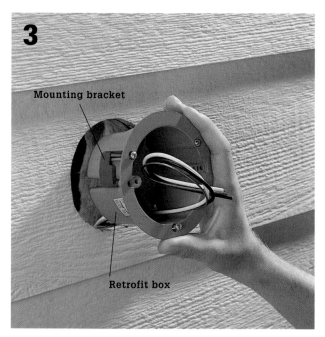

Mounting bracket

Retrofit box

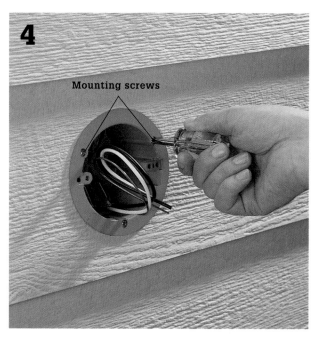

Mounting screws

Strip about 10" of outer insulation from the end of the cable using a cable ripper. Open a knockout in the retrofit light fixture box with a screwdriver. Insert the cable into the box so that at least ¼" of outer sheathing reaches into the box.

Insert the box into the cutout opening, and tighten the mounting screws until the brackets draw the outside flange firmly against the siding.

How to Replace a Floodlight with a Motion-Sensor Light

Turn off power to the old fixture. To remove it, unscrew the mounting screws on the part of the fixture attached to the wall. There will probably be four of them. Carefully pull the fixture away from the wall, exposing the wires. Don't touch the wires yet.

Before you touch any wires, use a voltage sensor to verify that the circuit is dead. With the light switch turned on, insert the sensor's probe into the electrical box and hold the probe within ½" of the wires inside to confirm that there is no voltage flow. Disconnect the wire connectors and remove the old fixture.

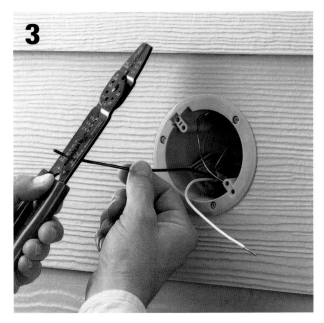

Examine the ends of the three wires coming from the box (one white, one black, and one bare copper). They should be clean and free of corrosion. If the ends are in poor condition, clip them off and then strip ¾" of wire insulation with a combination tool.

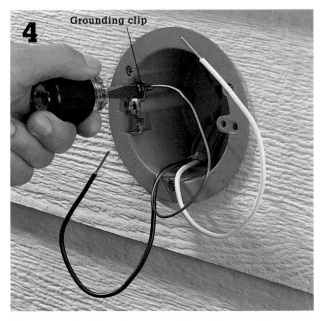

Grounding clip

If the electrical box is nonmetallic and does not have a metal grounding clip install a grounding clip or replace the box with one that does have a clip, and make sure the ground wire is attached to it securely. Some light fixtures have a grounding terminal on the base. If yours has one, attach the grounding wire from the house directly to the terminal.

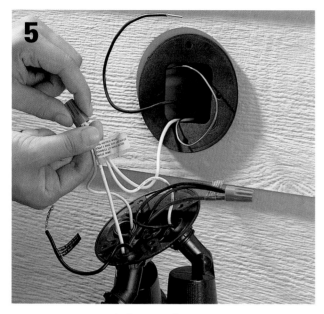

5

Now you can attach the new fixture. Begin by sliding a rubber or foam gasket (usually provided with the fixture) over the wires and onto the flange of the electrical box. Set the new fixture on top of a ladder or have a helper hold it while you make the wiring connections. There may be as many as three white wires coming from the fixture. Join all white wires, including the feed wire from the house using a wire connector.

6

Join the black wire from the box and the single black wire from the fixture with a wire connector. You may see a couple of black wires and a red wire already joined on the fixture. You can ignore these in your installation.

7

Neatly tuck all the wires into the box so they are behind the gasket. Align the holes in the gasket with the holes in the box, and then position the fixture over the gasket so its mounting holes are also aligned with the gasket. Press the fixture against the gasket and drive the four mounting screws into the box. Install floodlights (exterior rated) and restore power.

8

Test the fixture. You will still be able to turn it on and off with the light switch inside. Flip the switch on and pass your hand in front of the motion sensor. The light should come on. Adjust the motion sensor to cover the traffic areas and pivot the light head to illuminate the intended area.

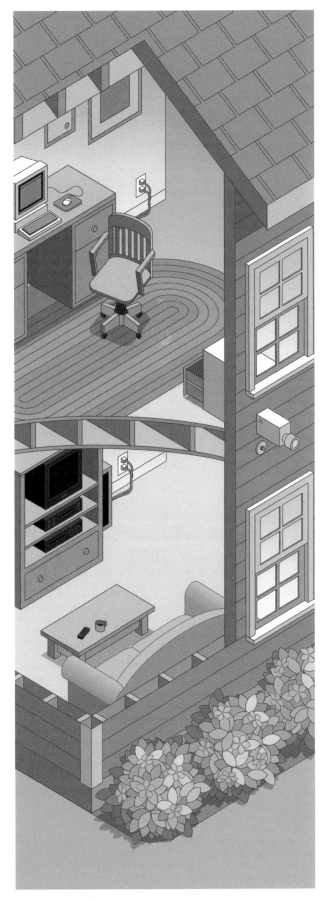

Multimedia outlets use modular jacks, connectors, and terminals to allow homeowners to customize outlets according to the network needs of each room.

Voice/data jacks can accommodate any pin-size telecommunication jack to allow for standard phone and data lines, or the ability to create multiline phone, data, and computer networks for the home office. Reassigning any line is quick and easy.

Accessories, such as closed-circuit cameras, allow homeowners to tailor the system to their specific needs.

Video F-connectors provide every room in your house with the ability to receive and redistribute antenna, cable TV, and satellite signals, as well as internal transmission signals from DVD, VCR, and closed-circuit cameras.

Audio terminals or a recessed speaker system can be installed for a home theater system or to create an internal audio system with localized volume control.

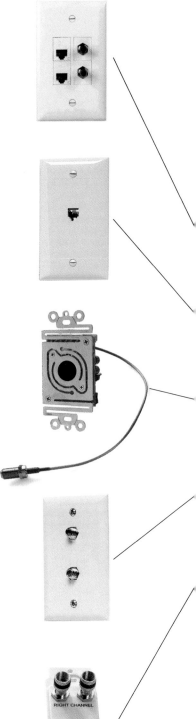

Installing a Home Network Wiring System

The ability to send and receive information electronically has become an important part of our lives. Internet access, multiple phone lines, cable television, satellites, wired and wireless home computer networks, and security systems are commonplace in many homes. And as our telecommunications needs grow, a better, faster, and more convenient way to manage these separate systems will be necessary.

A home network system brings all these single systems together at one central location. It provides a transmission path for electronic information rather than for electricity. Electronic information can be voice, video, audio, or computer data. Network wiring is about moving this electronic information to wherever you need it.

Older phone and cable TV wiring use a continuous loop wiring method. With this method, various jacks and connectors are installed along a single loop of cable or wire running throughout the house. Though easier to install, this method is unreliable, especially with the large demands placed upon the lines by computers and other electronic devices.

In this traditional method, the cable or wire that is split runs from the demarcation point, Network Interface Device (NID), or service entrance—the point where the service providers transfer ownership of the lines to the homeowner. The transmission signals are strongest at the point they enter the home. But repeatedly splitting cables and wires throughout the run degrades the strength of the signal. Also, if there is a problem in the line, all the jacks and connectors in the run are affected.

New home network wiring systems resolve this problem. The system employs a star topology in which all cables and wires are distributed from a central point. All inputs are brought to a centralized distribution center that contains modules designed to maintain the strength of voice, data, and video (VDV) transmission signals. High-performance cable and wires are routed to any room in the house where VDV capability is necessary. Plug-and-play multimedia outlets provide easy access to a variety of signals.

The system can be used to create home computer networks, multiroom audio systems, multiple phone lines for home offices, and distribution for DVD, DVR, VCR, or closed-circuit television signals to any room of the house.

Installing a system is a project that any homeowner can accomplish. Many home centers carry all the components and materials necessary for installation.

It is much easier to run cables and wires in unfinished walls, but retrofit installations are quite manageable if you carefully plan the system needs, determine the optimal location for each unit, and map out the cable routes.

Though installation methods and techniques for network wiring systems are generally the same, there are some differences between the different manufacturers' systems. Always carefully read and follow both the instruction and operation manuals provided by the manufacturer of your specific network wiring system.

Preparing Multimedia Outlets

Multimedia outlets are installed much like electrical receptacles, though the connections do not need to be contained in a box. The outlets should be mounted at the same height as receptacles, according to local code.

Extension brackets allow multimedia outlets and electrical receptacles to be placed side by side. The location of the 120-volt receptacle/switch box will always determine the height and location of the bracket. Make sure to choose the correct bracket for the outlet type to be installed. Some manufacturers offer specialized alignment tools for lining up the extension brackets with the existing electrical boxes.

For retrofit installations, hollow-backed gang boxes or 4 × 4" gang boxes are used to prevent damage to cables and wires due to bending or twisting.

Tools & Materials ▸

Level	Extension brackets
Screwdriver	Hollow-back boxes
Wallboard saw	Wallboard screws

Multimedia outlets can be installed next to electrical outlets in an expanded box, or installed in their own box.

How to Expand a Receptacle Box

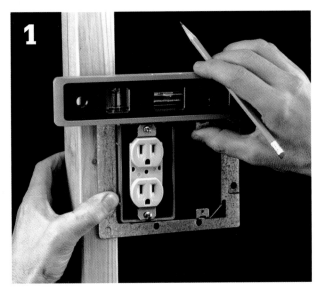

1

Fit the extension bracket over the existing electrical receptacle box. Align the bracket so that it is level and square and properly spaced from the existing box. Use an aligning tool, if provided, or a faceplate as a guide.

2

Fasten the bracket to the stud with two screws. The multimedia outlet box is then attached to the mounting ears on the extension bracket.

How to Retrofit a Single Multimedia Outlet Box

Use a wallboard saw to cut a hole at the outlet location that will accommodate the box size, a 4 × 4" gang box or hollow-back box, for a single outlet.

Route all the desired cables and wires to the distribution center location. Leave 12 to 18" of slack at each outlet location.

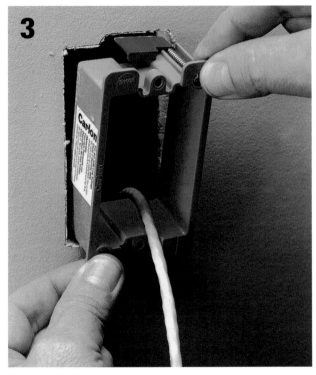

Thread all the cables into or through the gang box. Position the box in the hole.

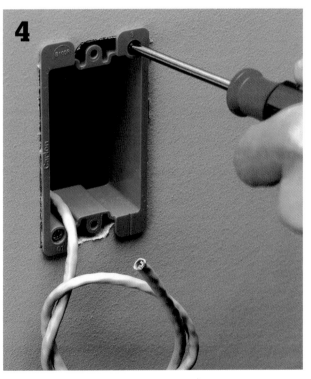

Tighten the mounting screws until snug to the wall. Avoid overtightening the screws to avoid damaging the wallboard.

Mounting the Distribution Center

Most distribution centers are designed to fit between standard stud spans of 16" on-center. For stud bays of different dimensions, you need to install blocking to support the distribution center. Retrofit installations require that you remove a large portion of finished wall and then refinish it once installation of the entire system is complete.

The bottom of the enclosure should be installed at least 48" above the floor. Most models require a ¼" gap behind the enclosure to accommodate the modules and fastening hardware. The front should protrude 1¹¹⁄₁₆" plus the thickness of the drywall from the studs to allow the cover to fit (depends on model).

A dedicated 15-amp, 120-volt electrical receptacle is suggested and may be required, depending on the grade of installation.

Tools & Materials ▸

Screwdriver
Level
Wood screws
Distribution center

Wood shims
Cable clamp
15-amp,
 120-volt receptacle

A distribution center organizes all the network controls in one spot.

How to Recess Mount a Distribution Center

Install the distribution center at least 48" above the floor. Position between two studs with a standard span of 16" on-center.

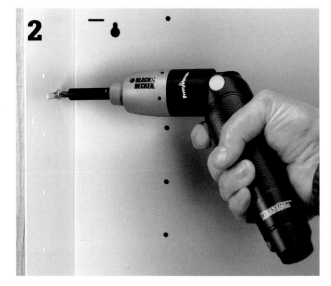

Use wood screws, one for each of the mounting slots located on the sides of the distribution center, to fasten to the studs. Do not fully tighten the screws.

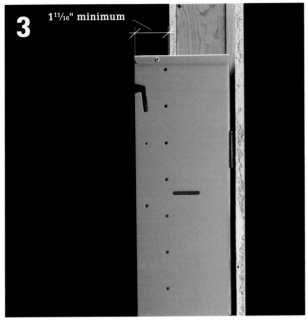

3 1¹¹/₁₆" minimum

Use wood shims to create a minimum ¼" gap between the back of the distribution center and the wall. The front edge of the center should protrude at least 1¹¹/₁₆" from the finished wall face. Adjust the shims for proper spacing, check for level, and tighten the screws to secure the center in position.

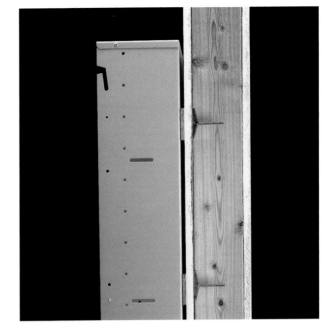

Alternative Method: Surface-mount the distribution center. Leave a ¼" gap between the back of the center and the wall. Use wall anchors where needed, with spacers or shims as necessary.

How to Install the Power Supply

Staple cable here

Run electrical NM cable in the bay next to the distribution center using cable staples to affix the cable to the stud. Drill a 1" hole through the stud into the adjoining bay 4" below the distribution center.

2

Feed the NM cable through the hole and into the gang box of the distribution center. Attach the cable with a cable clamp. Install a grounded 15-amp, 120-volt receptacle before completing the rest of the installation.

Routing Cables & Wires

Routing cable and wire of any kind requires drilling holes through framing members throughout the home. Drill holes no closer than 2" from the top or bottom edge of joists. Use nail plates to protect holes in studs within 2" of the edge. Always check your local building codes for requirements in your area.

Low-voltage cable can run a maximum of 295 ft. from the distribution center without any significant signal loss.

To route cables and wires, begin at the outlet bracket or box locations, and feed to the distribution center. The maximum allowable pulling tension for UTP cable is 25 pounds. Use electrical tape to hold the tips of all cables and wires together as they are fed, and avoid knots and kinks. Leave at least 12" of slack at bracket or box locations for making connections.

If your service connections are outside the home, drill 1" holes through to the outside near the service entrance location. Insert a 1" PVC conduit, and feed cables and wires through it. Leave 36" of slack, and attach notice tags to the ends for utility workers.

At the distribution center, mark each cable and wire according to its routing location. Feed each through the top of the enclosure, and cut the lead ends so they hang even with the bottom of the distribution center. When routing is complete, tuck all cables and wires neatly inside the distribution center and finish wall construction. For tips on routing cables and wires in finished walls, refer to page 60.

Tools & Materials ›

Drill	Tape
RJ45 crimp tool	Cables
F-connector	RJ45 plugs
Crimp tool	F-connectors

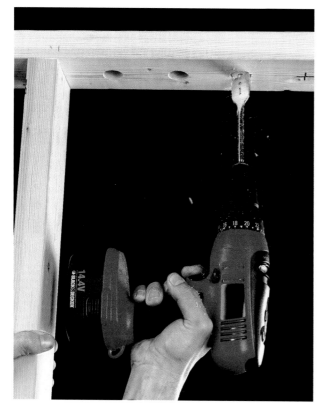

Drill 1" holes through the top plate above the distribution center. Drill holes in floor joists for running cable along the underside of house levels and from the service entrance to the distribution center.

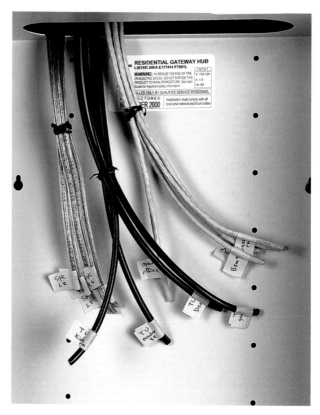

Label each run of cable and wire at the distribution center with the room and location within the room. All cables should hang even with the bottom of the distribution center.

How to Attach RJ45 Plugs to a UTP Cable

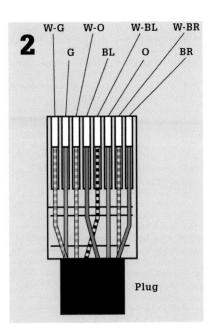

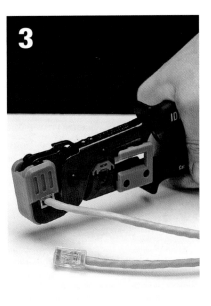

Strip 1 to 2" of outer insulation from the UTP cable. Separate the twisted pairs of individual wires.

Straighten and arrange each of the wires in order, according to the wiring assignment chart. Trim the ends evenly to ½" from the outer insulation. Insert the wires into the grooves of an RJ45 plug.

Make sure each wire is under the proper IDC (the conductor ends of the RJ45 plug) and that the outer insulation is ½" inside the plug. Crimp the plug with an RJ45 crimp tool.

How to Attach F-connectors to Coaxial Cable

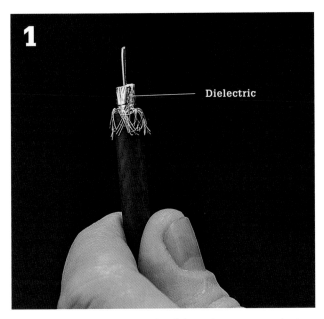

Strip the jacket and dielectric ⅜" from the center conductor. Strip the jacket ¼" from the foil and braid.

Slide the metal F-connector on until the dielectric is flush with center barrel. The center conductor should extend ¹⁄₁₆" past the end of the F-connector. Crimp the outer barrel of the connector to the cable jacket using an F-connector crimp tool.

Terminating Connectors

With the distribution center and multimedia outlets placed, and all the cables and wires routed, finish the walls in each room before terminating the connectors. Most connectors and jacks are designed to snap into the cover plate.

Any style of telecommunication plug will fit in an RJ45 jack. UTP cable is terminated to the eight pins of the jack in an industry standard configuration referred to as the T568A wiring standard. A 110-punchdown tool is used to terminate the wires to the corresponding terminals.

To terminate video connectors, crimp an F-connector to the coaxial cable end (page 119), and screw it to the backside of the self-terminating F-connector at the cover plate.

Tools & Materials ▸

Wire stripper
Screwdriver
110-punchdown tool

RJ45 jacks
F-connector
    terminals

Before terminating a connector, pull all cables and wires for all multimedia outlets through the cover plate, leaving 8 to 12" of slack for termination. Attach the cover plate in place with the screws provided.

How to Terminate an RJ45 Jack

1

Strip 2" of outer insulation from the UTP cable. Be careful not to cut through the twisted pairs within. Untwist each pair of individual wires.

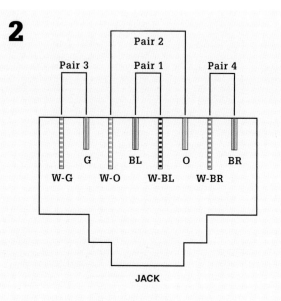

2

The back side of most RJ45 jacks are color-coded in the T568A wiring standard, so the proper colored wire from the UTP cable can be easily terminated to the proper terminal of the jack.

Place each wire into the groove of the appropriate terminal on the RJ45 jack, then use a 110-punchdown tool to seat the wire completely. The tool has a spring-tension head that forces the wire down and trims off the end. There should be no more than ½" of wire from the terminal to the outer cable insulation.

Fit a terminal cap over the ends of the jack terminals, then snap the jack into the cover plate.

How to Terminate Video Connectors

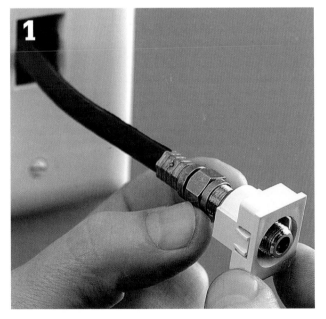

All coaxial video cables have plug-and-play connectors. The F-connector cable end is simply screwed to the back of the self-terminating F-connector terminal, and then snapped into the cover plate.

Video cameras also have plug-and-play self-terminating F-connector connections. Consult the manufacturer's installation guide for setup and playback of your particular camera.

Making Final Connections

To house the distribution modules, mounting brackets are installed within the distribution center. Some brackets and modules will require screws for installation, while others use plastic pushpin grommets.

For easy connection to modules, RJ45 plugs are attached to UTP cable ends and F-connectors to coaxial cable ends (page 120). All cables and wires should be clearly marked for easy identification and installation. It is best to keep all cables and wires routed to the same modules in neat, organized groupings. Bind the groupings with tie wraps where appropriate.

Once all the connections are made and the system is in working order, a cover is attached to protect the electronic modules and cable connections.

Tools & Materials ▸

Screwdriver
Modules
RJ45 plugs
F-connectors

Screws or pushpin
  grommets
  (as required)

How to Install Distribution Center Brackets

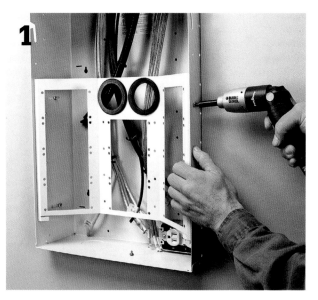

Attach the module mounting bracket to the distribution center. Align the mounting holes of the bracket panel with the prerouted holes in the sides of the distribution center and attach using the screws provided.

Attach any additional single brackets that may be necessary for specialized modules or for keeping power transformers separate. Some brackets require screws for installation, while others use pushpin grommets.

How to Mount & Connect Modules

1

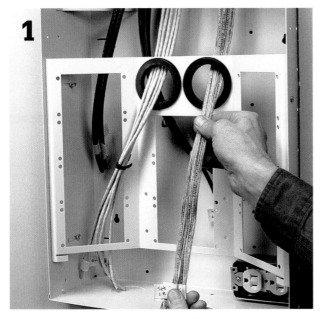

Determine where each module will be placed in the mounting brackets. Route any cables and wires through the mounting brackets to their corresponding module.

2

Plug the power transformer into the power distribution module, then snap the power module in place. The methods for module installation differ among network wiring manufacturers. Some require screws, while others use convenient pushpin grommets. Plug the power transformer into the 120-volt receptacle of the distribution center.

3

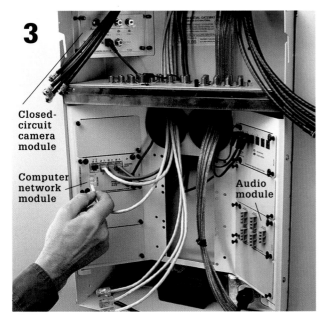

Use patch cords to connect the power module to those modules that require power, such as the video distribution, computer network, and video camera modules. Then install the remaining modules in their chosen locations.

4

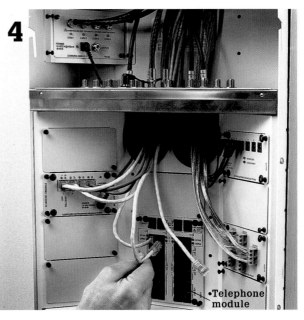

Trim the ends of all cables and wires, and attach the appropriate plugs or connectors. Refer to the labels to connect the proper cable to the proper module output port in order to route the desired function to the desired location. Make sure all cables and wires from the service entrance are connected to an input port.

Acknowledgements

Briggs & Stratton Power
800 743 4155
www.briggsandstratton.com

Broan-NuTone, LLC
800 558 1711
www.broan.com

Crossville, Inc.
931 484 2110
www.crossvilleinc.com

Cabin Fever
Cabins built in Miami, Florida
www.metroshed.com

Generac Power Systems
www.generac.com
www.guardiangenerators.com

Home Automation, Inc.
800 229 7256
www.homeauto.com

**Honda Power Equipment/
American Honda Motor Company, Inc.**
678 339 2600
www.hondapowerequipment.com

Hubbardton Forge
802 468 5516
www.vtforge.com

Ideal Industries, Inc.
800 435 0705
www.idealindustries.com

Ikea Home Furnishings
610 834 0180
www.Ikea-USA.com

Insinkerator
800 558 5700
www.insinkerator.com

Kohler
800 4 Kohler
www.kohlerco.com

Pass & Seymour Legrand
800 223 4185
www.passandseymour.com

SieMatic Möbelwerke USA
215 604 1350
www.siematic.com

Westinghouse
Ceiling fans, decorative lighting, solar outdoor lighting, &
other lighting fixtures and bulbs
800 245 5874
Purchase here: www.budgetlighting.com
www.westinghouse.com

Photo Credits

p. 47 & inset 51 (lower right) photo © Mike Clarke /
www.istock.com
p. 100 photo courtesy of Cabin Fever, featuring McMaster
Carr vapor-tight light fixtures

Resources

p. 78-79
Flatwire Surface-mounted Wire Tape
Southwire Company
800-444-1700
www.FlatwireStore.com

Index

Also From CREATIVE PUBLISHING international

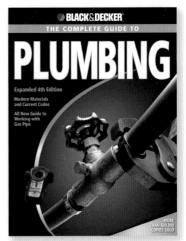

ISBN 1-58923-378-6

ISBN 1-58923-355-7

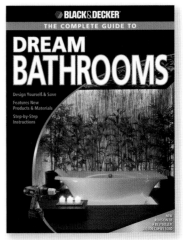

ISBN 1-58923-377-8

Creative Publishing
international

400 First Avenue North • Suite 300 • Minneapolis, MN 55401 • www.creativepub.com